THE CONCEPT OF BENEVOLENCE

New Studies in Practical Philosophy
General Editor: W. D. Hudson

The point of view of this series is that
of contemporary analytical philosophy.
Each study will deal with an aspect of
moral philosophy. Particular attention
will be paid to the logic of moral discourse,
and the practical problems of morality.
The relationship between morality and
other 'universes of discourse', such as art
and science, will also be explored.

Published
R. M. Hare *Practical Inferences*
R. M. Hare *Essays on Philosophical Method*
R. M. Hare *Essays on the Moral Concepts*
R. M. Hare *Applications of Moral Philosophy*
N. M. L. Nathan *The Concept of Justice*
R. W. Beardsmore *Art and Morality*
T. A. Roberts *The Concept of Benevolence*
Antony Flew *Crime or Disease ?*

THE CONCEPT OF BENEVOLENCE

Aspects of Eighteenth-Century Moral Philosophy

T. A. ROBERTS

Professor of Philosophy,
University College of Wales, Aberystwyth

MACMILLAN

First published 1973 by
THE MACMILLAN PRESS LTD
London and Basingstoke
Associated companies in New York Toronto
Dublin Melbourne Johannesburg and Madras

SBN 333 12055 8

Printed in Great Britain by
R. & R. CLARK LTD
Edinburgh

Contents

Editor's Foreword

In moral philosophy there has been a revival of interest in the problem of the *grounding* of morality. Illuminating and important as the achievements of modern philosophers have been in analysing the job, or jobs, which moral speech-acts characteristically perform, the vital question – or so it seems to many – remains, namely, 'What is the ultimate foundation of moral obligation?' Is the last appeal in moral argument necessarily to a consensus of moral commitment which happens to be shared by those participating in the argument, or is it to the moral tradition of the community within which the discussion occurs, or is it to something logically more fundamental than either of these, namely to facts about human nature as such? Because this question is in the air, Professor Roberts' study of three classical moral philosophers, who related their philosophical psychology very directly to their moral philosophy, will be of more than historical interest. Not only is it valuable as an admirably clear introduction to Hutcheson, Butler and Hume, but also for the light which it shows that these classical authors are able to shed on our contemporary concerns.

University of Exeter   W. D. HUDSON

Introduction

The relevance of the discussion of problems in philosophical psychology, or the philosophy of mind, to moral philosophy has been frequently emphasised in contemporary philosophy. Less frequently made is the claim that in eighteenth-century philosophy one can discover several examples of pioneering attempts to discuss problems in philosophical psychology which are of direct relevance to moral philosophy. However, apart from the philosophy of Hume, students of philosophy are not, in general, well acquainted with eighteenth-century philosophy. For this reason, this essay on the Concept of Benevolence focuses attention on discussions of benevolence which are to be found in the works of three British philosophers belonging to that century. These are Francis Hutcheson, Joseph Butler and David Hume. Discussions of benevolence figure prominently in the philosophy of all three. Moreover all three develop their philosophical psychology on the basis of very similar empiricist presuppositions, and although contemporary philosophy can no longer accept these presuppositions, their discussions, as this essay hopes to show, succeed in expressing valuable and relevant philosophical insights. Since it is confined to an examination of aspects of eighteenth-century philosophy, this essay is to be regarded more as a prologomenon to an analysis of benevolence than as an attempt at furnishing a fully developed analysis of the concept. Historical questions as to why discussions of benevolence became so prominent in the eighteenth century, or what influence this philosophical discussion had on practical philanthropy, are not discussed. Lack of space has precluded an examination of the more 'rationalist' approach of Kant to benevolence, to counterbalance the empiricism of the three British philosophers, Hutcheson, Butler and Hume.

1   Hutcheson on Benevolence

Francis Hutcheson, son of a Presbyterian minister, born and educated in Ireland where he was himself ordained a Presbyterian minister, was appointed Professor of Moral Philosophy at Glasgow University. He was a leading philosopher of the first half of the eighteenth century whose philosophical influence has led some to claim for him the title of 'the father of Scottish philosophy'. Whether this is justified or not, his main claims to fame are as the friend of, correspondent with and formative influence on the philosophical development of an incomparably greater philosopher, David Hume; as a significant precursor of Utilitarianism; and as a prominent figure in the philosophical controversies of his age, especially in ethics and aesthetics.

These controversies centred mainly, though not exclusively, on certain issues in moral philosophy. For example, one issue raised epistemological questions concerning the basis of moral judgements: are they based on 'perceptions of the moral sense', or derived from unaided reflections of reason? Another was the dispute between those who held that virtue consisted in actions motivated by benevolence and their opponents who denied the possibility of benevolent actions, and argued that human actions are motivated by selfish considerations. In the former dispute Hutcheson championed the 'moral sense' view, a term he borrowed from Shaftesbury, who was the first to use it. Although considerably influenced by Shaftesbury, Hutcheson went further than his teacher by developing a more complex and coherent version of the moral sense position. He assigns a prominent place in his moral philosophy to the notion of benevolence, and this chapter will be mainly concerned with his views on this subject. The discussion will be confined to his earliest, and perhaps best known, philosophical work, that is, the *Inquiry Concerning Moral Good and Evil*, which was the second of two treatises first published in one volume in 1725 under the title, *An Inquiry into the Orginal of our Ideas of Beauty and Virtue*.

Hutcheson's view on benevolence will be discussed as follows: his views on (i) the relation between benevolence and the moral sense, (ii) the nature of benevolence, (iii) the relation between self-love and benevolence and (iv) his arguments against egoism.

1. *The Moral Sense and Benevolence*

Hutcheson's moral sense theory is derived by extending a general empiricist epistemological thesis to the field of ethics and, on account of the similarities between them, to aesthetics. The general epistemological thesis is that all ideas are either simple or complex; that complex ideas are analysable into simple ideas; and that simple ideas are derived, directly or indirectly, from sense impressions. Extending this thesis to ethics, it is held that the fundamental notions of ethics and aesthetics – the good, the right and the beautiful – are simple ideas, derived directly or indirectly from sense impressions.[1] As moral ideas are not derived solely from impressions of the five sense organs – we cannot see, or touch, or hear goodness – the moral sense theory combines its epistemological thesis with a distinction, derived from Locke, between inner and outer sense. For Locke, inner sense is 'reflexion', that is to say, the mind's power of reflecting on its own states of mind. According to Locke, there is no genuine analogy between inner and outer sense and therefore he did not develop the idea of an inner sense, or senses, which are non-cognitive in character.[2] Hutcheson however maintains that there exist distinct impressions or perceptions of inner sense (or senses for there may be more than one of them), as there exist perceptions or impressions of outer sense. The correspondence between outer and inner sense is not precisely the same, for the impressions of inner sense are secondary, in a way that impressions of outer sense are not; that is, the existence of impressions of inner sense presupposes the existence of perceptions of outer sense, which are, for this reason, primary. Apart from the secondary nature of the perceptions of inner sense, the perceptions of the inner and outer senses are on all fours. In particular both sets of perceptions are given, are underivative and are 'mysterious' in the sense that their existence as a brute fact in human experience is something ultimately inexplicable. It is possible to argue that there are causal connections between the existence of the perceptions of inner and outer sense on the one hand, and the physical and physiological structure of human nature on the other hand, but we are unable, in Hutcheson's view, to state what these causal connections are, nor will it ever become possible to do so. It is thus characteristic of Hutcheson's approach to ethics that he seeks to ground it in what he takes to be the empirical facts about human nature, and his ethical conclusions are offered as the fruit of the inductive method applied to morals.[3]

In the class of perceptions which belong to inner sense, Hutcheson includes the 'passions, affections and sentiments'. Then in order to account, on his empiricist presuppositions, for our capacity to make moral and aesthetic judgements, he singles out a particular set of 'affections and sensations' which furnish the raw material upon which the judgements or deliverances of the moral and aesthetic senses are based. Thus if at a particular moment one is very angry one is the victim, in Hutcheson's terminology, of a 'passion', and the state of mind of being angry or of feeling anger is a 'particular perception'. From our experiences of such particular perceptions we form the simple idea of anger, an idea which enters necessarily into a judgement such as, 'I am now very angry'. Of course, it does not in the least follow from my saying that I am angry that I am in fact having the kind of experience which Hutcheson calls a particular perception, identifiable as the experience of being angry, for I may say that I am angry in order to pursuade others to believe that I am angry, when in fact I am not. But it is normally presupposed by my saying or uttering the words 'I am now angry' that I understand what 'anger' is and that I can correctly identify states of mind, either my own or those of others, which are to be correctly described by expressions involving the concept of anger.* For Hutchseon, one can understand a concept such as anger only if it is derived from experiences of particular instances of states of mind describable as states of mind of being angry or of feeling anger. Such states of mind, such inner mental perceptions, are brought into exist-

* It is necessary to qualify this contention with the word 'normally' because it is clear that in some contexts a person who says or utters the words 'I am now angry' does not understand what the expression means.

ence as a result of our having mental experiences of another sort, namely perceptions of outer senses, that is, perceptions of objects existing outside us. Thus if I see (that is, have 'perceptions of outer sense' in Hutcheson's terminology) a man beating a dog into insensibility, these primary perceptions of outer sense may give rise, or 'raise' (Hutcheson's term), perceptions of a particular sort which belong to inner sense; that is, I may experience perceptions or states of mind describable as states of being angry. My anger may become so strong that I may, in my frenzy, be led to attack the man in the hope of stopping him beating his dog. Such anger would be called a passion by Hutcheson, with the suggestion in the use of that term that to experience a passion is to experience emotions or feelings so deep that they may lead a man to act violently towards other human beings, animals or inanimate objects.

How is this example related to Hutcheson's views about the moral sense? Perceptions of objects which are at the same time perceptions of outer sense arouse in us perceptions of inner sense which are perceptions of these objects as pleasurable or painful to us, implying the corollary that every object we experience is experienced as either pleasurable or painful. Thus, if I see a fire, my seeing the fire (a series of perceptions of outer sense) arouses the perception or idea* of inner sense which is the awareness of the fact that fire can be painful if it burns any part of my body. Equally, seeing a fire can rouse the awareness that fire can give my body warmth, and this experience of being warmed by a fire is pleasurable. That external objects can cause us to experience states of mind which are either pleasurable and agreeable or painful and disagreeable is for Hutcheson a fact which is so because human beings possess a human nature structured in a particular way. Indeed, for Hutcheson, God has created human nature in such a way that these things are so.[4]

As perceptions of 'objects' of outer sense can lead to our having perceptions of inner sense, so also the outer-sense perception of actions or events can arouse a set of perceptions of inner sense which are distinctive enough to be classified as (inner) perceptions of the moral sense. Thus if I see a young lad

---

* Hutcheson loosely uses the word 'idea' sometimes to mean the same thing as the expression, 'particular perception', i.e. a state of mind, and sometimes to mean the concept which is based upon our having experiences of particular sorts of states of mind and their contents.

shepherding a blind man across the road, I have perceptions of outer sense. But these perceptions of outer sense can give rise to distinctive perceptions of inner snese. This happens if what I see is perceived or 'apprehended' as a good (or bad) action, for this apprehension gives rise to a perception of the moral sense, that is, I experience 'the perception of approbation'; in other words, in the presence of what I judge to be a good action I experience a state of mind which is describable as one of 'feeling approval', and this state of mind is a pleasurable experience. Conversely if I observe a bad or evil action I feel disapproval, and this state of mind is painful or disagreeable. Moverover the pleasurable feeling or sentiment I experience when I have the perception of approbation, or the painful feeling or sentiment I have when I experience the perception of disapproval or 'condemnation' (Hutcheson's term) are not derived from intellectual calculations that the actions so approved or disapproved will be to my interest or advantage, or to my disadvantage. Thus Hutcheson offers as one of his definitions of the moral sense: 'We mean by it only a Determination of our Minds to receive the single ideas of Approbation or Condemnation, from Actions observ'd, antecedent to any opinions of Advantage or Loss to rebound to ourselves from them . . . .'[5]

In introducing the example of a young boy shepherding a blind man across the road, it was stated that if this action was 'perceived' as morally good by an observer, he would experience a 'perception or sentiment of approbation'. In Section II of the *Inquiry* Hutcheson introduces a discussion of the motives or springs of actions, and in particular discusses the motives of virtuous actions. In this section he makes clear that to 'perceive' or 'apprehend' an action as a morally good action requires consideration not only of the external action – that is, a particular change in that state of affairs (or, in certain contexts, a failure to bring about a certain change in the state of affairs) – but also of the motive from which the agent performs the action. A motive Hutcheson terms 'an affection'. Thus he writes, 'every action, which we apprehend as either morally good or evil, is always supposed to flow from some Affection toward sensitive natures; and whatever we call Virtue or Vice, is either some such Affection, or some Action consequent upon it'.[6] Those affections which motivate men to act morally are therefore very important The cardinal virtues – courage, temperance, prudence, justice –

are in fact 'dispositions universally necessary to promote publick good', and their names denote 'affections towards rational agents'.[7] Hutcheson asserts that the most important affections in morals are those which are included under 'the names Love and Hatred'. Love towards rational agents is subdivided into 'love of complacence or esteem, and love of benevolence'. Complacence or esteem denotes 'approbation of any person by our moral sense and is rather a perception than an affection'.[8] Benevolence is an affection and is defined as 'the desire of the happiness of another'.[9] The opposites of complacence and benevolence are said to be dislike and malice.

We are now in a position to survey the relation between the moral sense and benevolence in Hutcheson's *Inquiry*. First it is the moral sense which enables a man to perceive or apprehend a morally good (or bad) action. The good action is good because it is motivated by a moral motive. All moral motives can be subsumed under benevolence, that is, an affection that seeks as its object the good of another. This good Hutcheson equates with the individual's happiness. From the standpoint of the observer, when he perceives or apprehends a morally good action (that is, an action motivated by benevolence) he experiences a 'perception of an approbation' towards the agent, and this in turn 'raises' in him 'an affection of good will' towards him, which may in turn be what motivates the observer to act benevolently, and so act morally, towards the agent. From the standpoint of the agent, he acts morally when he seeks to bring about a state of affairs which constitutes the happiness of another and does this not from motives of self-interest nor from any other motive save that of seeking the good of another, the good being understood in terms of his happiness.

The close connection between benevolence and the moral sense in Hutcheson's thought is immediately apparent from this summary. So far as the notion of a moral sense is concerned, we can readily appreciate the force of the analogy Hutcheson seeks to elaborate between perceiving an object by means of the outer sense, and 'perceiving' or 'apprehending' an action to be good or bad by means of the moral sense. The analogy is far from satisfactory, its most obvious weakness being the fact that human beings do not seem to possess the necessary faculty for moral sensing as they do possess sense organs which are instruments of outer sensing or perception. Nevertheless, despite its limitations, it serves Hutcheson's purpose well enough, for it allows him to use it to express two strongly held convictions about morality, one concerning the objectivity of moral judgements and the other concerning their non-rational character. The moral-sense notion is a model developed to substantiate a claim that my judging something (a person or an action) to be morally good is very like ordinary perceptual (and therefore empirical) judgements about the world, as when I judge an object to be red. The element of similarity Hutcheson wishes to establish between moral and perceptual judgements turns on the fact that a moral judgement ascribes a quality of goodness to a person or event (as when I say of a person or of an action that it is good) which I 'apprehend' in the person or action, just as my claim that an object is red is the claim that that object possesses the 'quality' or property of redness. In either case, if I wish to judge correctly, I cannot choose not to call the action or person good nor the red object red. Ascribing goodness to persons or actions or ascribing redness to red objects is not for Hutcheson a matter which is within the discretion of the will. Granted an object is red, and granted that I possess the sense of sight normal to human beings, I am 'determined'; that is, human nature being constituted as it is, I must see the object as red. I can choose to *say* that it is not red but I cannot choose to *see* it as not red. Similarly, human beings are so constituted that they *must* respond to benevolent actions or benevolent persons in the way Hutcheson has described: they experience perceptions of approbation, which in turn give rise to affections of goodwill towards benevolent actions or persons, and these affections, granted the existence of appropriate conditions or circumstances, may then operate in the spectator to make him become a moral agent who acts benevolently.

The second function which the moral-sense model seems to perform is to express Hutcheson's belief that perceiving or apprehending goodness or badness is not an intellectual process but one which is to be described in terms of the special 'perceptions, sentiments and affections' which belong to the moral sense. In maintaining this viewpoint he was of course disagreeing fundamentally with the rationalist or intellectualist thinkers who followed Samuel Clarke in believing that apprehending or perceiving moral qualities was the work of certain intellectual processes of which human beings were capable. Hutcheson and the intellectualists were in general agreement about the 'objec-

but on Hutcheson's view, the approval is not *moral* approval.

Benevolence is said by Hutcheson to be an affection. The question can be raised whether Hutcheson thinks benevolence is a distinct affection in addition to the four affections of compassion, love, gratitude and humanity with which he closely associates it, or whether it is a name for these four affections, and not a separate fifth affection to be named 'benevolence'. On the whole it seems Hutcheson held the former view: benevolence is a distinct affection.

What does the term 'affection' mean for Hutcheson? When predicated of a mental state, as it is always meant to be by Hutcheson, 'affection' stands for that mental state which is initially brought into existence by something acting upon the mind. No affection, in Hutcheson's view, can be 'raised voluntarily'. Neither 'benevolence nor any other affection or desire can be directly raised by volition'.[14] That is, a person cannot choose to have the affection of benevolence, to feel good-will towards someone, as he can choose to imagine something or other, or as he can choose to have thoughts on topics of his choice. If it were possible voluntarily to 'raise' affections, then, according to Hutcheson, a man might be bribed to feel good-will towards his neighbour. Now it might be thought that Hutcheson is suggesting that one of the criteria for a mental state being an affection is that it cannot be summoned into existence by an act of will, as a thought or an image can be. However, Hutcheson is not offering this criterion as a general criterion of affections, but only as one of the criteria of the affection of benevolence, and perhaps also of the 'kind affections' (compassion, love, generosity, humanity), for he concedes that some affections can be 'raised voluntarily' by an act of will. Such affections are those which serve as motives for actions which are in our self-interest or to our advantage, and they can be summoned into existence through an act of will by concentrating the mind's attention on those qualities of the objects of these affections which are of interest or advantage to us. Since benevolence does not in the least involve considerations of our interest or advantage, it cannot be one of the affections which can be directly 'raised voluntarily'. Although the affection of benevolence cannot be 'raised' in us by an act of will, Hutcheson does not wish to deny that we can choose, by an act of will, to desire to be benevolent. Such a denial would be unfortunate, for men do sometimes desire to be benevolent. Such desires lead us to concentrate on certain aspects of events or persons (for example, the generosity of a generous person) and this attention may lead to the affection of benevolence being 'raised' in us, but the desire to be benevolent is not the cause of the affection of benevolence arising in us: nothing can cause it to arise in us but the perception of the appropriate qualities of objects or events.[15] It does seem that, in one passage at least, Hutcheson allows that the affection of benevolence can be indirectly raised in us by an act of will, whereas previously he had implied that only affections involving our interest could be so indirectly raised voluntarily. To this extent it appears that Hutcheson's views are not altogether consistent on this topic.

By saying of an affection that it is a state of mind which cannot be directly 'raised voluntarily' by us, Hutcheson wants to stress the fact that the existence of such a subjective state of affairs is contingent upon the presumed existence of certain objective states of affairs, that is, upon the existence of 'qualities' in objects or events. If this is so, an affection, although a mental mode, is not a mode of the understanding, for it is characteristic of the understanding that it is spontaneous, and can within certain limits freely bring into existence the objects of its attention. An affection is not therefore something brought into existence by an intellectual process, although the recognition of an affection as a state of mind of a particular kind (e.g. benevolence) may involve an intellectual process. If an affection is to this extent non-intellectual, or non-cognitive, it belongs to those states of mind which are predominantly states of emotion or feeling.

By calling benevolence 'a calm affection' Hutcheson contrasts the feeling tone of the affection of good-will with the uneasiness or restlessness which he implies accompanies every desire, and with the potential violent manifestation of every passion. Affections, desires, passions are all emotive states of mind (that is, non-intellectual), but they differ in the degree of emotion involved.

For Hutcheson the highest perfection of virtue springs from 'a universal calm good will'. The use of 'universal' in this expression must presumably refer to the object of the affection, that is, those who are 'affected' by those actions motivated by the affection of universal calm good-will. If a man, either in word or deed, acts generously towards us, this 'raises' in us the affection of good-will towards him, a state of mind which in turn can motivate our actions for his good. The man who acts generously towards others acts from the motive of good-will towards others, and this motive may become a settled disposition of character which inspires or motivates reflected acts of generosity. For Hutcheson it is 'natural' for a man to act from such a settled generous disposition towards his nearest and dearest, and towards those in the circle of his closest friends. But it is possible, and this is an attainable perfection to be striven for, that the circle of those to whom we are generous should be so enlarged as to embrace everyone. A man who feels good-will towards everyone possesses 'the universal calm affection of good will towards all'. Thus for Hutcheson the affection of benevolence is 'natural' in the sense that men do feel good-will towards those who do them acts of kindness, as they feel good-will naturally towards their own friends. In this sense most men are benevolent. But it is possible for each man to aspire towards the perfection of possessing benevolence towards all, irrespective of whether they are his friends or relatives. Universal good-will is not natural in the sense that all men possess it, but it is natural in the sense that nothing in a man's nature prevents him from developing and acquiring it, and the frame of human activity is conducive to its development. The highest virtue is not just benevolence but benevolence towards enemies and love of the worst characters.

A further criterion of the kind affections in general, and of benevolence in particular, is disinterestedness. That is, if a person acts from good-will towards another, there must be no thought of gain to himself from the action. This does not rule out the possibility that a man may gain pleasure or satisfaction from acting benevolently towards others, but it does exclude the possibility that he deliberately intended, by his action, to gain advantage for himself. Hutcheson points out that compassion towards others involves associating ourselves with the suffering and distress of others, and this is not pleasant, and so disproves the contention of those who argue that benevolence is 'interested' in the sense that the agent always experiences pleasant feelings when he acts benevolently.

To understand what it is to act disinterestedly from a motive of good-will it is useful to consider by contrast what it is to act from motives other than good-will, for example acting maliciously. Hutcheson considers the question whether malice is the exact opposite of benevolence in the sense that there may be 'disinterested malice', as there is unquestionably for him 'disinterested benevolence'.[16] He concludes that always associated with malice is the thought of some gain or advantage to the agent flowing directly or indirectly from his malicious deeds. We intend to harm people from whose discomfiture we stand to gain. It is not clear whether Hutcheson is contending that it is logically impossible to be malicious without associating it with thought of personal gain or interest, or whether he is saying it is contingently the case that in human nature as we know it, malice is never disinterested, which leaves open the possibility that in another world malice may be on occasion disinterested. By contrast with malice, that benevolence is disinterested is a remarkable and significant fact. In making this claim about benevolence, Hutcheson seems to be stating what he thinks is a fact about human nature, rather than establishing a logical point about the concept of benevolence, to the effect that if an action is intentionally 'interested', then that action cannot (logical cannot) be an act of benevolence.

We can act from selfish motives as well as from the motive of good-will to others. That is, we can attempt to bring about states of affairs which we believe are beneficial to the self, irrespective of whether such actions are either beneficial to others or positively harmful to others. We can perform actions which we know or believe will do harm to others because we intend that they should do good to ourselves. This differs from malice, where the harm done to others is intentional and deliberate. In very selfish actions, our powerful selfish tendencies make us 'careless of the sufferings of others', or in seeking our own good we may be 'negligent of the good of others'.

Finally we must note Hutcheson's discussion of the relation between benevolence and moral worth. If the criterion of all virtue is benevolence, then we must judge a man's moral worth by the degrees of benevolence expressed in his actions, so far as we are able to assess it. However, an assessment of a man's moral worth is not solely a matter of assessing the degree of his benevolence, for according to Hutcheson moral worth is compounded of 'natural abilities and benevolence'.[17] Men naturally differ in their natural abilities and capabilities. Where natural abilities are equal, moral worth will differ on the basis of the degree of benevolence expressed in their actions. Where natural abilities are unequal it may be easier for the man who possesses greater natural abilities to act more benevolently than another possessed of lesser abilities, so that if they both produce the same amount of good, by their respective actions, the latter will be adjudged to possess greater moral worth.

Hutcheson is undoubtedly making a valid point here when he stresses that an assessment of moral worth has theoretically to take account of a man's abilities, as it has to take account of his circumstances, which may or may not be favourable, a point not made by him. But Hutcheson assumes what is disputable, namely that the sole criterion of virtue is benevolence, and whilst stressing the need to take account of a person's natural abilities in assessing moral worth, he does not attempt to lay down the criteria by which such an assessment is to be made.

On Hutcheson's discussion of the nature of benevolence we can offer this general comment. While his discussion illuminates many features of the notion of benevolence, his main strength is to have illuminated what benevolence is by reference to the affections of compassion, love, generosity and humanity, and to have developed his analysis of benevolence by contrasting what it is to act benevolently with what it is to act maliciously or selfishly. His main weakness is that he has failed to elaborate his analysis by considering what compassion, generosity, humanity and love are, how they differ from each other and how yet they are all instances of benevolence.

3. *Benevolence and Self-love*

In language reminiscent of Joseph Butler, Hutcheson states categorically that all men have both self-love and benevolence: 'All men have self-love, as well as benevolence, these two principles may jointly excite a man to the same action, and then they are to be considered as two forces impelling the same body to Motion.'[18] By self-love Hutcheson understands all that is to the advantage or interest of the self. He does not distinguish as Butler does between 'immoderate self-love' and cool or reasonable self-love, that is, he has no notion of those actions which are to the short-term benefit of the self, but may be harmful in the long run.

In Section II he argues against two different forms of the argument very prevalent in his day, that benevolence is a variant of self-love, that we act for the good of others because this brings some gain to the self.

The first thesis is that 'we voluntarily bring the affection [of benevolence] upon ourselves whenever we have an opinion that it will be for our interest to have this affection, either as it may be immediately pleasant, or may afford pleasant reflections afterwards of our Moral Sense, or as it may tend to procure some external reward from God or Man'.[19]

Hutcheson's main argument against this thesis is one to which reference has already been made, namely that no affection can be 'raised' by an act of will, and that therefore we cannot will into existence the desire for the happiness of others even though the fulfilment of such a desire brings us pleasure or satisfaction. There are, however, further considerations which weigh against this thesis.

First, it is not true that benevolence is always accompanied by pleasure.[20] Hutcheson's example is compassion, for in showing compassion to others we are invariably involved in feeling pain at their distress and affliction.

The second objection is that it is not true of any desire or affection that the desire or affection 'terminates upon the pleasure which may accompany the affection'.[21] This is another way of saying that the object of an affection – in the case of benevolence, achieving the happiness of others – is not the same thing as the pleasure or satisfaction which the agent obtains when this object is achieved.

Another objection rests on an appeal to introspection. This shows, according to Hutcheson, that we do possess the desire for the good of others 'generally without any consideration or intention of obtaining these pleasant reflections on our own virtue'.[22] Introspection reveals this most clearly when we examine our love towards our parents or offspring, or our attitude towards someone who has been generous towards us.

Hutcheson deals at some length with the claim that a desire for eternal reward for the self is what really motivates our actions for the happiness of others. It is possible, he concedes, to do good to others both from a motive of disinterested benevolence and from a desire for eternal reward, but the fact that both motives can lie side by side does not destroy the case for the view that we sometimes act from the sole motive of disinterested benevolence.[23] As for the motive of seeking the happiness of others from a desire to be rewarded by God in the next life, we cannot approve of actions done solely from this motive for the simple reason that we would not approve of someone acting from this motive in obedience to an evil deity, nor indeed would we approve of someone acting from this motive in obedience to a good deity, unless the motive was accompanied by love and gratitude towards the deity. Now love and gratitude imply disinterestedly seeking the good of those whom we love or those to whom we show gratitude. Therefore we cannot approve someone who does good to others from the sole motive of seeking eternal rewards for the self.

Hutcheson then examines the second thesis, which he regards as much the more plausible of the two. This is the thesis that 'the observation of the happiness of other persons, in many cases is made the necessary occasion of pleasure to the observer, as their misery is the occasion of his uneasiness: and in consequence of this connexion, as soon as we have observed it, we begin to desire the happiness of others as the means of obtaining this happiness to ourselves, which we expect from the Contemplation of others in a happy state'.[24]

In a quotation echoing Malebranche, to whom he refers more than once in the *Inquiry*, Hutcheson gives expression to the view that there is a necessary connection between the happiness of others and one's own happiness, such that the existence of the former is invariably accompanied by the existence of the latter.

This view does not imply what is false, namely that the happiness of others is the cause of my own happiness or that the happiness of others is a necessary condition of my happiness. The invariable and regular relation observed to hold between the happiness of others and the happiness of the self leads us to desire the former in order to achieve the latter; that is, the happiness of others is desired as a means to our own happiness. To this thesis Hutcheson offers the following objections:

1. We do not approve someone desiring the happiness of others simply as a means of procuring wealth or sensual pleasure for himself. Hutcheson's example to support this contention is the

case of a man who bets 'concerning the future happiness of a man of such veracity that he would sincerely confess whether he were happy or not'.[25] We would surely not approve of a man who would wish another man's happiness in order to win a bet and so benefit thereby.

2. Appealing once again to introspection,[26] we discover that when we act for the happiness of others we intend to bring about their happiness, but the desire for our own pleasure or happiness is not part of that intention. While it is true that their happiness will give us pleasure or satisfaction, what we intend or aim to bring about is their happiness and not the pleasure this gives us. Here Hutcheson anticipates a distinction for which Butler has often been given credit for being the first to make.

3. Hutcheson reminds us that it is a fact that after death we feel neither pleasure nor pain but this does not obliterate the anxieties and hopes we feel at the point of death for the well-being of our friends and relations.

4. Finally Hutcheson considers the view advanced by some that to desire the happiness of others necessarily involves our own pleasure, for any desire implies uneasiness, and to achieve the object of the desire removes this uneasiness; and this is to give us pleasure.

Hutcheson replies to this by pointing out that we need to distinguish between a desire and the uneasiness we feel until and unless the desire is fulfilled. Although closely connected these two are not the same thing, as extension and colour are not the same, although the idea of extension is closely related to the idea of colour. Likewise the object of desire is one thing and the satisfaction of fulfilled desire is another, but we do not aim at the former as a means of obtaining the latter.

Besides discussing these two main contentions concerning the relation of self-love to benevolence, Hutcheson offers further interesting observations on this subject. He notes, for example, that the motives for action are mixed, and that it is possible for self-love and benevolence both to be motives of the same action. In other words there is no necessary incompatibility between self-love and benevolence.[27] He contends that in general vice is motivated by a mistaken view of self-love, which becomes too strong for benevolence, for rarely is an action motivated solely by a desire to do evil.[28] This idea is somewhat similar to

Butler's notion of 'immoderate self-love' although Hutcheson never formally makes this distinction. He implies however that, within its limits and in the right context, self-love is a perfectly acceptable motive for action: acting from self-love is consistent with striving for the good of the whole and Hutcheson believes the principle of self-love to be indispensable.[29] By drawing an analogy with the principles of mechanics in physics, an analogy which he does not elaborate upon, Hutcheson talks of the 'moment of good' in any action as being a function of the motives of benevolence and interest which are responsible for its existence. Thus 'the amount of good' in an action performed from motives of benevolence and interest would be as high as in an action performed from benevolence alone if in the former case the strength of benevolence was such that the action would have been performed even if the motive of interest or advantage, attributable to self-love, had not been present. This implies the possibility of being able to state the criteria for assessing the respective strengths of motives such as benevolence and interest, and Hutcheson does not attempt to specify these criteria. It also implies the appropriateness of thinking of motives as forces of varying strength which operate one upon another as is the case with physical forces in mechanics.

4. *Benevolence, Interest and Advantage*

At the end of his Introduction to the *Inquiry* Hutcheson states that the contents of his work are devoted to establishing two propositions, namely, (*a*) that we give moral approval to some actions without consideration of the natural advantage that may flow from them to us; and (*b*) that the intention of actions which gain moral approbation is not an intention to gain 'sensible pleasure' for the agent, much less to gain future rewards based on divine laws. The intention of such actions is 'based on a principle of action entirely different from self-love or desire for private good'.

In Section I of the *Inquiry* Hutcheson considers counter-arguments against the first proposition. The second proposition is in effect covered by his discussion of self-love.

What Hutcheson has in mind by the expression 'natural advantage', which he uses in the first proposition, must be briefly discussed. In the Introduction he observes that we distinguish between moral and natural good. Natural goods consist of such things as houses, lands, gardens, vineyards, health, strength and sagacity. Examples of moral goods are honesty, faith, generosity and kindness. In Hutcheson's view 'we necessarily love and approve the possession of moral goods', though this is not true of natural goods. The validity of the distinction between moral and natural good is further borne out by our reaction to moral and natural evils respectively. Moral evils such as treachery, cruelty and ingratitude arouse dislike, whereas natural evils – pain, poverty, sickness, hunger and death — arouse our pity and compassion for those who suffer from them. The natural advantage which flows from actions is what increases, or tends to increase, natural goods for us.

In Section I Hutcheson proceeds, not very systematically, to review some considerations for and against the view that we only approve what is to our interest or advantage.

First, we are all conscious of the distinction between moral approval (based on benevolence) and non-moral approval of natural goods. If we were not so conscious of this distinction, how explain that our 'affection towards' fruitful fields or commodious habitation is different from our affection towards a generous friend or a noble character, although both the fruitful field and the generous friend may be of equal advantage to us? Moreover we would not admire a noble person in a distant country whose influence cannot extend to us if approval was grounded on consideration of what is to our advantage or interest. Nor would we distinguish between the 'sentiments' we have towards inanimate objects, which may be beneficial to us, and our sentiments towards just and benevolent persons. We do not equally approve both, and this is on account of a 'distinct perception of beauty or excellence' in the kind affection of rational agents, 'whence we are determined to admire and love such characters and persons'.

To show that moral approval is not based on considerations of advantage, consider the case of our benefiting equally from two actions, one done from a motive of benevolence, and the other from a motive of self-interest in the agent.[30] Our 'sentiments' of the two actions would not be the same, and this proves that perceptions of moral actions are not based on advantage. Equally, our motives of moral evil are not based on considera-

tions of advantage, otherwise we would react in the same way
to the moral ends of 'assault, buffet, affront from a neighbour'
as to the natural evils such as 'fall of a beam, tile or tempest', in
circumstances where these actions are equally disadvantageous
to us. 'Villany, treachery, cruelty would be as weakly resented
as a blast, mildew, or an overflowing stream.' In any case, we
react most strongly by way of anger and indignation to those
evil actions which we believe to be motivated by hatred, even if
those actions are in no way disadvantageous to us.

Hutcheson then tackles a number of counter-assertions in
favour of the view that all approval is based on considerations
of advantage.

1. The first is the assertion that all the actions we approve in
others are believed 'to tend to the natural good of mankind, or
some part of it'. Since the approver is part of mankind, his
approval of the action of others is approval for what benefits
him as part of mankind. To this line of argument Hutcheson
retorts by asking how can one connect the approver's interest
with his approval of what occurs in distant parts of the world.
When he first considers this notion that approval is of what is
for the natural good of mankind, Hutcheson does not develop
his objection. He merely implies that it is difficult to see how an
individual's interest is to be related to the consequences of
actions approved in distant parts of the world, and that to say
all approved actions tend to the natural good of mankind does
not allow us to make the connection, because the expression
'natural good of mankind' is too indefinite to enable us to forge
the link. Later[31] he returns to a similar assertion, namely to the
argument that whatever profits one part without detriment to
another profits the whole, and therefore some small share will
accrue to the individual. Thus those actions which tend to
the good of the whole best secure individual happiness, and
so we approve them because of 'their tending ultimately to
our advantage'. To this Hutcheson replies by asking rhetori-
cally – what advantage do we reap from Orestes' killing the
treacherous Aegysthus? The only concession he makes here is
to suggest that we immediately approve some actions in others,
and later rational reflection reveals these actions are to our
advantage.

In dealing with this objection Hutcheson does not distinguish
between the claim that actions morally approved of tend to the

moral good of mankind and the quite different claim that what we approve of tends to the *natural* good of mankind, and that this is the basis of all approval. What is clear is that Hutcheson wants to support the former and reject the latter, but his rejection of the latter is made in terms of a quite different problem, namely, if we say that approval is always of actions which tend to the *natural* good of all, how is this justified in terms of the view that all approval is based on what is to the individual's advantage? In short, the difficulty of relating the individual's advantage to the notion of the natural good of all becomes a reason, in Hutcheson's opinion, for rejecting the view that all approval is based on calculations of natural good.

2. One objection to the claim that approval depends on considerations of the approver's interest or advantage is based on the fact that we approve actions performed in the distant past. But this approval of past actions can be justified by the defender of egoism on the grounds that 'we approve or condemn characters according as we apprehend we should have been supported, or injured by them, had we lived in their days'.[32] To this Hutcheson replied that if our approval of past actions is based on calculations as to whether such actions would have benefited us, then we have no reason for not approving the evil of tyrants and traitors if their deeds had been advantageous to us. But we do not approve a miser as we approve a hero, though a miser's money will be advantageous to his heir. Why is this? 'It is plain that we have some secret sense which determines our approbation without regard to self-interest', otherwise we would always approve what favours us without regard to virtue.

3. One way of countering the thesis that approval is grounded on advantage is to consider whether it is possible for an observer to perceive moral good and therefore approve an action which is disadvantageous to him personally. Hutcheson argues for this possibility by way of an example which contrasts the case of the refugee and the 'resolute, burgomaster'.[33] The refugee flees his country on account of persecution and settles in another which he benefits by establishing a flourishing and prosperous trade on the basis of specialised skills he brings with him. The resolute burgomaster stands fast in his own country and wages 'perilous war' against his tyrant ruler, forms a republic which in time becomes prosperous and rivals our own country in trade. Which of these two characters do we most

admire? 'Let every man consult his own breast, which of the two characters he has the most agreeable Idea of? whether of the useful refugee, or the publick spirited burgomaster, by whose love to his own country, we have often suffered in our interests... He will find some other foundation of esteem than Advantage.'

4. We must distinguish between the desire to do what is virtuous and our perception of the beauty of what is virtuous either in actions or in character.[34] We can be seduced from the desire to do our duty by considerations of what is in our interest. Thus a man can be tempted by bribes not to do what is virtuous or to do what is vicious. But can any bribe make us approve a wrong to a minor or orphan, or ingratitude to a benefactor? We may be bribed by hope of reward to do iniquitous things but the bribes do not persuade us that we approve what we are bribed to do.

5. From the above distinction between the desire to do virtuous things and our approval of virtue, it becomes clear on reflection that if we judged actions solely by the criteria of their advantage or disadvantage to ourselves, we would not be able to choose an action because it is to our advantage, while being conscious of its evil or wrong nature. The fact that we do sometimes consciously choose to do what is wrong, knowing it to be wrong, because the action is believed to be to our advantage, presupposes the conceptual distinction between judging what is believed to be to our advantage and judging what is believed to be virtuous by criteria other than what is to our advantage.

6. Hutcheson considers a theological argument for thinking that all approval is based on calculations of advantage.[35] We approve what is good because we believe God will reward all good action, and thus all approval is ultimately grounded in calculations of what is to our advantage. Hutcheson further considers arguments grounding moral approval on divine goodness in Section II, paragraph vii. Here in Section I he is content with two contrary observations. First, that men who have no belief either in God or in a good God nevertheless possess moral notions of honour, faith, generosity and justice. Secondly, considerations of future divine reward and punishment may make my own actions appear advantageous to me, but such considerations would never make me *approve* actions by another based solely on such considerations. Beliefs concerning possible future divine rewards and punishments may, like bribes,

influence my *desire* to do what is virtuous but they cannot be the ground of the approval of what is virtuous, for I do not approve in others actions motivated mainly by considerations of divine reward or punishment.

7. Hutcheson reviews two considerations advanced by Mandeville ('a late witty author') in his *The Fable of the Bees* in favour of basing approval on interest or advantage.

(i) Quoting Mandeville, Hutcheson outlines the first consideration. 'Leaders of mankind do not really admire such actions as those of Regulus, but only observe, that men of such dispositions are useful to the defence of any state.'[36] The state inculcates in its citizens, by means of education and propaganda, a readiness to praise what is useful to the state, and what is praised is what is approved. What is approved thus rests on what is useful. To the thesis that we approve what is useful, Hutcheson counters by pointing out that we distinguish between a traitor and his acts of treachery. If the treachery is beneficial or advantageous to our country, we approve of the traitorous actions but we disapprove of traitors. 'We love the treason but hate the traitor.' This moral condemnation of the traitor cannot therefore be based on consideration of advantage, for we only approve those of his actions which are advantageous.

As for the contention that men praise what is advantageous, and approve what is praised, Hutcheson replies to Mandeville's reference to Regulus by observing:

(*a*) that Regulus did not benefit from what he did, only his country: therefore if what is praised is identical with what is advantageous, Regulus cannot have praised what he did: that is, he did not admire or approve what he did, even though it benefited his country. Since there is something odd about this conclusion, the premise that we only praise what is advantageous must be suspect;

(*b*) Regulus could not, on Mandeville's argument, praise or approve the acts of another hero which did not benefit him, and this is again a strange conclusion to reach;

(*c*) what could make Regulus desire praise for his actions if the criterion of praise for an action is 'the cold opinion of others that the action is useful to the state' with no assessment of the excellence and virtue of such conduct?

(ii) The second contention[37] derived from *The Fable of the*

Bees, which Hutcheson seeks to demolish, is the view that the state for its own purposes can so regulate by law the behaviour of its citizens that they come to feel there is such a thing as a public good, that this is excellent, and that they admire actions for the public good by others and imitate such actions in themselves, thereby forgetting the pursuit of their own advantage.

It is, replies Hutcheson, far more than law can accomplish, and in any case, is a task far more difficult than Mandeville has recognised, to get a person who is thoroughly selfish to imagine others to be public-spirited. We are asking law and statutes to convince a person who has no idea of goodness, other than what is to his own interest, by the example and persuasion of others to adopt a conception of the good which is detrimental to himself and beneficial to others. This 'is more than statutes and panegyricks can accomplish'. 'It is an easy matter for men to assert anything in words but our own hearts must decide the matter.'

We have reviewed in this section the many points which Hutcheson brings against the view that moral approval is grounded on considerations of self-interest. As was stated at the outset, these arguments are not very systematically presented nor are they fitted into one comprehensive, tightly argued chain of argument. Moreover in the final paragraph of Section I Hutcheson lets slip a remark which all but undermines his opposition to basing moral approval on self-interest: 'The author of nature . . . has given us a moral sense to direct our actions, and to give us still nobler pleasures; so that while we are only intending the good of others, we undesignedly promote our own greatest private good.'[38] This view is undoubtedly inconsistent and at variance with the main drift of the points Hutcheson has advanced for rejecting the view that moral approval is based on advantage and interest. Its presence here adds credence to the view that Hutcheson's thought in the *Inquiry* is neither fully thought-out nor completely consistent. On the one hand he was perceptive enough to be able to recognise the strong arguments against a position such as that adopted by Mandeville. On the other, the empiricist epistemology he took over from Locke led him to develop the notion of a moral sense, and it is from this notion of the moral sense that he is led to contend that 'moral perceptions' are always attended by special and heightened perceptions of pleasure. From this it is only a small step to argue that we act morally in order to enjoy these distinctive feelings of pleasure. Hutcheson vigorously denies this very contention, but it is one to which the logic of the moral-sense notion irresistibly leads. What Hutcheson has failed to see is the incompatability between the full logical implications of adopting the notion of a moral sense or faculty and his own on the whole rational, sane and wholly acceptable distinctions in morality such as the view that moral approval is not based on interest or advantage.

2 Benevolence in Butler's *Sermons*

Born on 18 May 1692 at Wantage in Berkshire, the son of a retired linen draper, Joseph Butler was educated at the Dissenting Academy at Tewkesbury in Gloucestershire and later at Oriel College Oxford, a college he entered as a commoner in 1715. On leaving Oxford he was ordained in the Anglican Church where in the course of his career he held several ecclesiastical appointments, including the Deanship of St Paul, before being preferred to the see of Bristol in 1738. In 1750 he was appointed Bishop of the Diocese of Durham, a see he was to preside over for only two years before his death in 1752.

Bishop Butler is best known for his *Fifteen Sermons*, first published in 1726, a collection of sermons delivered at the Rolls Chapel in London, and for his *Analogy of Religion*, a substantial, sustained 'thorough and painstaking countering of objections to natural theology and to the Christian revelation'.[1] The *Analogy* has deservedly gained considerable influence amongst theologians; two important and influential figures who have acknowledged their debt to Butler are Cardinal Newman and, in recent times, Bishop Kirk of Oxford. The *Fifteen Sermons* has also attracted the interest and respect of philosophers on account of its systematic discussion of certain aspects of moral philosophy, a discussion expressed in language which is invariably chosen with great care, being always as precise and as rigorous as the subject-matter demands. The very economy and tautness of Butler's prose style may not appeal at first reading but on close acquaintance it commands respect and admiration for the great skill and clarity with which he succeeds in making fine and subtle distinctions, as is demanded of any fruitful discussion of moral philosophy.

1. *Butler's Philosophical Method*

Butler's views on benevolence cannot be fully appreciated unless they are set in the general context of his thought. In the Preface to the second edition of the *Fifteen Sermons*, a preface written mainly to rebut the charge of obscurity levelled against him by his critics, and to summarise the main drift of his arguments, Butler contends that the subject of morals can be studied in either one of two ways. One can begin by 'inquiring into the abstract relations of things' or one can start from a matter of fact, namely, 'what the particular nature of man is, its several parts, their economy, or constitution'.[2] Butler adopts the latter empirical approach, rejecting the *a priori* method of reasoning from 'the abstract relation of things', which was characteristic of the rationalist or 'intellectualist' school of thought led by Samuel Clarke (1675–1729), an Anglican divine, a close friend of Isaac Newton, and a man whose theological and philosophical ideas seem to have been considerably more influential in his day than has been generally appreciated. Despite a close friendship with Clarke, who must have considerably influenced his own thought, Butler adopted the empirical method of the 'sentimentalists' such as Shaftesbury, who is mentioned by Butler in the Preface to the *Sermons*, and Francis Hutcheson. Butler's main aim in making the analysis of human nature the central theme of his moral philosophy was to underline the Stoic dictum that 'virtue is natural, and vice unnatural'. In concentrating attention on human rather than on the divine nature, Butler, in common with his contemporaries, reflects the significant shift in eighteenth-century thought from the more theological preoccupations of the previous century.

In his analysis of human nature Butler does not deal with the whole nature of man, physical and mental, but only with those features of mind or consciousness which he believes are essentially involved in man's moral behaviour. He did not, for example, set out to analyse, as Locke did, the nature of 'understanding', what constitutes the similarities and differences between knowing, believing, reasoning, remembering, imagining and dreaming. Rather Butler is content to confine himself to the more restricted task of attempting to state what those 'principles and propensities' of human nature are which motivate men to act in this way rather than that, and to discover the relations that hold between such principles and propensities. Since morality is pre-eminently concerned with certain aspects of man's behaviour, how we ought or ought not to behave, Butler thinks that the sure foundations of morality cannot be established without a clear understanding of what is involved on the side of consciousness in deliberate, intentional, purposive action. In general, morality is concerned with those actions which we deliberately do, or fail to do, and is not concerned with those of our actions which can be called reflex or unconscious, or those done under the influence of drugs or hypnotism. Such actions are not directly the subject matter of moral judgements. Butler is thus concerned primarily to give us an analysis of the part played by desires and motives in the purposive actions of human beings. What he wrote certainly conveys the impression that he thought he was engaged in a factual enquiry, a form of psychological investigation, a voyage of discovery into the realm of mind to report on some, if not all, of the qualities and attributes of mind there observed. Whereas Locke, a greater philosopher than Butler, if only because his philosophical speculations range far wider, attempted the formidable task of constructing a complete psychology of mind, Butler set himself the humbler and more limited task of setting out the essentials, as he believed, not of the psychology of mind, but of the psychology of mind in relation to moral action.

Historically the work of both Locke and Butler can be viewed in this light, for it is true that philosophical speculation in the seventeenth century, continuing into the eighteenth, reflects a new psychological shift of emphasis discernible in its concern to establish the nature and limits of the mind's powers of understanding. In so far as these speculations represent a genuine striving to establish a new science from which modern psychology as we now know it took its rise, to that extent they can be regarded as constituting the first chapter in the history of modern psychology. But to the philosopher they hold an interest that is more than historical. If it is legitimate to distinguish between a factual or empirical investigation on the one hand and a conceptual enquiry or analysis on the other, the philosopher's concern is more with the latter than with the former. The significance the philosopher assigns to the thought of Locke and Butler derives not only from its undoubted historical value but also from the fact that Locke's views are best under-stood as important, if frequently mistaken, attempts to offer conceptual, not factual, solutions to a cluster of problems in the psychology of mind, while Butler offers conceptual and not factual solutions to a more restricted range of problems in the philosophy of moral action.

2. *The 'Real Nature' of Man*

Butler begins his analysis of the various elements which he believes constitute that restricted part of human nature with which he is concerned by discussing the 'passions, affections and appetites', and the part they play in good conduct, which is natural, and in evil conduct, which is unnatural. Before examining Butler's account of the part they play in natural and unnatural conduct, the sense which is to be given to that obviously vague word 'natural' must be established for, as Chesterton long ago reminded us, some conduct can be 'more natural than it is natural to be'.

A person who acts on the passion, appetite or affection – understanding by these terms for the time being a certain general class of human motives or desires – that happens to dominate him at a particular moment, acts naturally, for in one sense of 'natural' everything that happens is a part of nature. But clearly this sense of 'natural' will not do if we wish, as Butler does, to establish the proposition that virtuous con-duct is natural, for we act virtuously not when we act from *any* passion, appetite or affection whatsoever but only when we act on the right passion, appetite or affection. Another sense of 'natural' is apparent when we say that a man acts naturally when he acts in character, that is, not in accordance with the dominant impulse of the moment but in accordance with the dominant tendencies of his character. But this second sense of 'natural' must also be rejected, for virtue does not rest in acting in accordance with the dominant dispositions of one's char-acter but in acting in accordance with right or virtuous dis-positions or tendencies of character.

Butler suggests a third sense of 'nature' which he believes is the one required to establish the meaning of the expression, 'virtue is natural'. For him, reflection soon convinces us that the 'principles and propensities' which motivate deliberate, purposive behaviour are hierarchically organised. The two criteria for classifying these elements in a hierarchical order are strength and authority. Each principle or propensity is said to possess, in the scheme of nature, the strength appropriate to its place and station in the hierarchy, and some principles and propensities possess greater authority because of their superior status in the hierarchy. Thus in Butler's completed analysis, the 'passions, affections and appetites' are assigned the lowest status, and to them belong the strength 'proportionate' to that status. However, in actual human nature, a man may act on a passion, affection or appetite whose strength is disproportionate to its status within the economy or constitution of human nature. To act in this way would be 'unnatural', and the action would be immoral. To quote Butler, 'the correspondence of actions to the nature of the agent renders them natural: their disproportion to it, unnatural'.[3]

Butler's analysis of human nature rests on certain presuppositions which need to be noted. First, he assumes that there is a norm or standard to which human nature in general conforms, although in particular individuals this common human nature may be distorted so that it deviates from the norm or standard. He refers to the norm or standard as 'the real nature of man' or 'the real proper nature of man'.[4] The notion of a 'real nature of man' as a common measure by which we can judge or assess the actual nature observable in particular individuals in turn implies certain assumptions. It implies, for example, that although individuals differ in certain respects, yet in general human beings resemble each other to the extent that they share a common nature, physical and moral. Most men are able to see because they possess eyesight. Even though individuals differ in the quality of their eyesight – some are short-sighted and some are long-sighted – and even though some individuals have never been blessed with eyesight or, once possessing it, have since lost the capacity to see, yet the majority share this characteristic in common – they are able to see and are not blind. Similarly most men know what it is to feel disgrace, and agree disgrace is to be avoided as much as pain, even though one set of circumstances may create a greater feeling of disgrace in one individual than in another, and there may be, exceptionally, an individual who never feels disgrace in any circumstances whatsoever. Thus to feel disgrace in certain circumstances is natural, and not to feel it in similar circumstances is unnatural.

In his proposed analysis of 'the real nature of man' Butler confines his attention exclusively to the moral, and not to the physical, qualities or characteristics of this nature. But by analogy with the physical, he adopts a teleological approach in his descriptions of these moral qualities. The organs of sight, i.e. the eyes, possess certain functions; they enable human beings, in the appropriate conditions of light, to see things, for if the eyes do not function properly, one cannot see.[5] Similarly the moral qualities or characteristics of our real nature exist to serve certain purposes, or certain purposes more than others. The fact that they do so serve certain identifiable purposes is a reason for thinking that this 'real nature of man' is the product of deliberate design, in fact the work of God who is 'the author of our nature'. This fact implies that it is possible to judge whether a particular 'faculty or power' of our real nature is being used properly, by considering whether it is being used for the purpose it was designed for. 'The due and proper use of any natural faculty or power, is to be judged of by the end or design for which it was given us.'[6] Thus Butler is Aristotelian in adopting a general teleological approach in his analysis of human nature, and is at one with the Schoolmen in linking this teleology to his Christian theology.

In Butler's view God has endowed man, so far as his moral capacities are concerned, with a 'real nature' which is designed to achieve certain moral ends or purposes. However, certain individuals, owing to the disproportionate strength of a particular passion or desire, may act in ways which 'violate their real proper nature',[7] and so act unnaturally, and immorally. What is the difference between 'real proper nature' and violated human nature? Butler answers by invoking the metaphors of harmony and disharmony, of authority and its opposite, rebellion. In 'real human nature' there exists a harmony between the different principles and propensities so that action motivated by passion, affection or appetite is always subservient to the superior and supreme principle of conscience. 'Our real nature leads us to be influenced in some degree by reflection and conscience.'[8] Our real human nature is thus amenable to rational influences and persuasion. Violated human nature on the other hand is dominated by disproportionately strong passions and desires, and its actions are irrational because performed in opposition to the dictates of reason and conscience.

Is Butler's notion of the 'real proper nature of man' equivalent to some notion of ideal human nature, as C. D. Broad suggests?[9] If by 'ideal' is meant some notion of perfect human nature, endowed with human qualities conceived as perfect, then Butler's 'real nature' is not ideal in this sense, for, true to his Christian theological beliefs, Butler frequently stresses the frailty and imperfection of the human frame and constitution. Butler's 'real nature' is man's nature as God has created it, so designed to achieve certain divinely ordained purposes. But this 'real nature' might have been constructed otherwise than it is. For example man's real nature is such that he suffers bodily pain as well as being capable of enjoying pleasure. But God could have created for man a more perfect or ideal nature which never experienced bodily pain, and indeed he could have endowed such an ideal nature with other perfections. But God did not choose to do so, but has given man a 'real nature' which is, in the circumstances of this world in which man actually finds himself, best adapted to fulfil his aims. Incidentally the theological doctrine of the Fall can best be harmonised with Butler's distinction between real and violated nature not by maintaining that the imperfections of real human nature are due to the Fall, but by insisting that the tendency in man to violate his 'real nature' through succumbing to disproportionately strong passions is a consequence of the Fall.

There is another reason for thinking that Butler did not equate 'real human nature' with ideal human nature. The notion of ideal humanity is derived from listing all those qualities and characteristics which men ideally should possess. The concept of such an ideal person, possessing all the possible perfections of our humanity is without application to a single instance, for no ideal individual person actually exists. The notion of the ideal thus becomes a norm or standard by which we express the moral values to which men ought to aspire. Contrary to this, Butler believes that his concept of the real nature of man is one derived from and based upon actual experience. This concept can have, and probably does have, application to particular instances; that is, it is in Butler's view a fact that there exist some individuals in whom conscience is allowed to exercise rightful authority over the various passions, affections and appetites constitutive of human nature. It is also an empirical fact for Butler that the concept of violated human nature has application, for there exist individuals who act in defiance of what conscience commands.

3. 'Appetites, Passions and Affections'

Critics have claimed that Butler does not explain his use of the terms 'passion, appetite and affection', and that the best that can be said in his defence in this connection is that his use of them implies a sharp distinction between 'appetite' on the one hand, and 'passion and affection' on the other, the latter two being used more or less as synonyms.[10] As the role Butler assigns to benevolence in the constitution or economy of human nature raises the question whether benevolence is a particular affection, it is necessary to examine carefully his use of these terms, for it is certainly true that Butler never explicitly discusses or indicates how he proposes to use them.

First let us ask what in Butler's analysis can be said in general of 'the passions, appetites and affections' as a class of motivating principles in human nature, before we proceed to seek differentiations between sub-classes within the general class.

They are, as a class, as much part of human nature as our five senses. Secondly, in themselves, 'our appetites, passions, senses in no way imply disease, nor indeed do they imply deficiency or imperfection of any sort'.[11] The constitution of our nature as God has made it require their existence: they are necessary to 'the imperfection of our nature'. This imperfection arises from the fact that a (particular) passion and (particular) affection, as 'distinct from a principle of reason, may rise too high and be beyond its just proportion'.[12] God could have created a human nature endowed with affections and passions which did not rise too high beyond their just proportion. Another source of imperfection may lie in the kind of passions, appetites and affections 'real human nature' actually does possess, for again God might have created 'a real nature' which lacked some of its present appetites and passions, such as resentment, but clearly such a nature would be very different from the 'real nature' Butler believes God gave man.

The 'passions, appetites and affections' share in common the characteristic that there exists a prior suitableness between them and their objects, which are external. As Duncan-Jones has pointed out, Butler offers no kind of analysis of the relation between a passion, appetite and affection and its object, nor does he consider the possibility that some passions and appetites may have internal objects. Neither does he analyse the distinction between internal and external objects, for Butler appears to rely on an unanalysed common-sense notion of 'object', regarding the relation between a passion, appetite or affection and its object as the single relation of possession, whereas in fact a variety of relations may hold between them.[13] Moreover the passions and appetites and affections for Butler afford the best example of final causes, for the existence of passions and affections lead, in appropriate circumstances, to 'a certain determinate course of action suitable to those circumstances'[14] in which they have been aroused, as for example when compassion is aroused it leads to action which relieves the distress of another, or of others.

4. *Appetites*

Butler says less about the specific nature of the appetites than he does about the passions and affections, although he does not say a great deal directly about the latter either. Perhaps the reason for this is that there is not a great deal that can be said in general about the appetites, though of course the analysis of the concept of a particular appetite, e.g. hunger, is quite a different matter. It was not however Butler's aim to discuss the general nature of the appetites, much as we might regret that he has not devoted more attention to indicating how he would have distinguished between an appetite, a passion and an affection.

Butler's examples of appetites are hunger, which is in certain circumstances a strong desire for food, and thirst, a strong desire for drink; the desire for sexual gratification is also an appetite. Now if we take hunger to be the strong desire for food which is aroused when one has been deprived of food for very long, we can ask, how does this desire differ from a desire for food which might arise in quite different circumstances? That is, how do appetites differ from desires which are not to be described as appetites?

Appetites seem to differ from other desires in at least two respects. First, there is some relation of dependence between certain physiological states of the body and those states of mind which are to be described as 'appetitive desires' or appetites. Thus if a person is well-fed, the appetitive desire for food does not arise. One of the necessary conditions of being hungry is to have been deprived of food for a considerable period of time. This is not a sufficient condition, for a man may not have taken food for a long while and yet he may not feel hungry because he is ill, suffering from a particular illness one of whose characteristic symptoms is loss of appetite. If a lack of food is a necessary condition of being hungry, then it follows that one cannot choose to feel hunger at will. A man fed regularly and plentifully cannot choose at will to feel hunger. Under those conditions he just cannot feel hunger, and this is a logical 'cannot'. Thus the appetitive desire for food which we associate with being hungry differs from the desire for food, or more accurately, a desire for a particular kind of food, which might arise in circumstances when one is not feeling hungry, as when the sight or the thought of a particular food can arouse the desire for that food.

Another feature of appetitive desires is that they are necessarily related to states of the self, whereas other desires may be, but are not necessarily, related to states of affairs of the self, as I can desire your well being which may include relieving your hunger. But in satisfying my hunger I am always doing something which changes my state of affairs, from one of being hungry to one of being fed or well-fed. Butler states that appetites resemble passions in that they terminate in an object. As Duncan-Jones points out, Butler is here falling back on the less precise language of common sense, as when we say that the object of hunger is food. More accurately, each appetite has as its objective a certain state of affairs. The objective of the appetite 'hunger' is a state of affairs in which, having taken food, a man is no longer hungry. Obtaining and eating the food are means to achieving this state of affairs. When I am hungry, what I seek to satisfy is *my* hunger, that is, the objective is a certain state of affairs of mine. It is impossible for me by taking food to satisfy your hunger, nor you by taking food to satisfy my hunger. In contrast to this, there are some desires I have which are mine whose objectives are states of affairs of others, as for example my desire to relieve your hunger.

A further characteristic of the appetitive desires is that they are connected, directly or indirectly, with our physical survival. The body cannot function if it is not given adequate nourishment of food and drink. A certain minimum quantity of food and drink is necessary for the health and physical well-being of the body, and lack of food and water over a comparatively short period leads to starvation and death. The minimum quantity of solids required for health is probably smaller than we, with our common-sense notions, fondly imagine, and ordinarily a person's intake of food is much greater than is strictly required for good health and well-being. A regular supply of liquid seems to be a more important requirement, for death follows much more quickly if a man is denied drink. In the case of the sexual appetite, its gratification is not an essential condition of the survival of the individual, as is evident from the comparative longevity of celibate nuns and priests. But it is clearly an essential condition of the survival of the race that some individuals gratify their sexual appetitive desires.

Butler holds that it is true of the appetites as well as of the passions and the affections that they can be gratified in particular instances without being 'subservient to the particular chief end, for which these several principles were respectively implanted in our nature'.[15] If the gratification of a particular appetite does not conflict with the 'particular chief end' of man, or with any moral obligation, its gratification is innocent. To follow Butler's thought here, we must decide what in his view constituted the particular chief end of man. Butler believed that man was created to seek the good of society, an end or aim not necessarily incompatible with seeking his own true good. Thus he conceives the possibility that a man could satisfy his hunger without thereby injuring the good of others. For example, in the New Testament, we learn of the disciples of Jesus walking through a cornfield on a Sabbath, and eating the ears of corn because they were hungry. Satisfying hunger in this manner is innocent, in Butler's view, provided it is not possible to accuse the disciples of injuring thereby the farmer's good by damaging his crops. And in this particular gospel example, such a charge would be difficult to sustain.

This leads to another of Butler's points concerning the innocence of gratifying appetites. One may satisfy an appetite provided that in so doing this does not conflict, or is not incompatible with, a moral obligation. I may seek food to satisfy my hunger provided I do not transgress a prior moral obligation, as for instance, the obligation not to steal either the money to buy the food or the food itself. Does this mean that a hungry man ought to starve to death rather than steal food or money so that he can relieve his hunger? The apparent harshness of such a view is softened by the fact that others have obligations to see that a hungry man does not starve. In any case the possible conflict between satisfying an appetite and a prior moral obligation can be seen as a clash between conflicting moral obligations, for each individual has a moral obligation, other things being equal, to sustain his life. Butler's discussion of appetites – or rather his lack of such a sustained discussion – falls a long way short of the recognition that in certain circumstances the gratification of an appetite may involve a conflict of moral obligations, and he says nothing as to how such conflicts are to be resolved. Satisfying desires for food and drink to the extent necessary to ensure the survival, health and well-being of the body are moral obligations, falling within the category of duties to the self. The gratification of sexual desires, however, since they are not necessary to the survival of the individual, cannot be regarded as forming part of the duties to the self. It might be argued that the satisfaction of sexual desires form an essential part of the 'well-being' of the self but this clearly turns on one's notion of 'well-being'. The fact that sexual desires are not on a par with the appetitive desires for food and drink must serve to remind us that the notion of an appetite is neither as simple nor as straightforward as one might originally suppose, and that it may be a vain enterprise to seek to establish a general analysis of 'appetite' which holds without qualification of all appetites, a point perhaps overlooked by Butler when he slips all too easily to talk of 'appetites, passions and affections' without distinction or qualification.

Butler states that 'every affection, as distinct from a principle of reason, may rise too high and be beyond its just proportion',[16] and the idea expressed in this quotation is evidently crucial to his conception of human nature as a hierarchically organised system in which some elements are superior to others. Unnatural, and therefore on Butler's view immoral, conduct issues from a desire which has 'risen beyond its just proportion', being in conflict with some superior principle of human nature. Now Butler sometimes uses the word 'affection' to stand without distinction for the class of motives, i.e. the passions, appetites and affections which motivate human actions; at other times he uses 'affections' in a more strict or narrow sense to refer to what one may loosely call desires, which are to be quite definitely distinguished from the appetites on the one hand and from the passions on the other. If the use of 'affection' in the above quotation is understood in its wider sense, it would be true of the appetites that they can 'rise and be beyond their just proportion'. Indeed it is an essential feature of Butler's analysis that each factor in the constitution of human nature may generate a strength greater than is its due, and thereby serve to motivate immoral or vicious conduct, and the appetites are a clearly distinct factor or element in the constitution of human nature. Butler does not however develop or elaborate upon the notion that an appetitive desire can rise beyond its just proportion; he does not, for example, consider what it would be for hunger 'to rise beyond its just proportion'. Since we are now engaged in trying to see how Butler would develop his distinctions between appetites, passions and affections, it may be worth exploring briefly the notion of an appetite rising beyond its just proportion.

The word 'proportion' implies strictly a numerical relation holding between two things or factors, and to qualify 'proportion' with the adjective 'just' implies the proportion is judged right, correct or valid; this in turn presupposes a reference to a norm or standard by which the proportion is so judged to be right, correct or valid. Now to talk of the appetite of hunger rising beyond its just proportion does not make it immediately evident whether the relation is to hold between the intensity of the desire for food which one feels when one is hungry and the length of the period one has experienced the hunger, or whether it holds between the intensity of the desire for food on the one hand and the quantity of food one takes to satisfy this desire. On the former possibility, if the interval without nourishment is judged to be T hours, the 'just proportion' might justify a desire of x degrees of intensity, whereas a desire of y intensity would count as an instance of a desire rising beyond its just proportion. On the second possibility, an interval of T hours without food could give rise to a desire of x intensity to be satisfied by z lbs of food, and if w lbs of food were consumed, this would indicate a desire which had arisen beyond its just proportion.

There is little point in pressing the question as to which of these possibilities Butler would favour. He does not discuss the subject of the nature of the appetites at any length at all, and so there is no means of knowing whether either of these two possibilities of interpreting the notion of 'just proportion' when applied to appetites occurred to him, or which of them he would favour. If one had to hazard a guess, one would choose the former. There are serious difficulties with both interpretations. For example, if the 'proportion' is understood strictly numerically, it presupposes that the intensity of the appetitive desire for food is quantifiable. It is however difficult to see how the intensity of desires can be measured; this is not merely connected with the fact that in practice we do not seem able to measure the intensity of desires, but it raises the question whether the expression, 'intense desire', even when associated with specifiable sensations as is the case with hunger, is a description of a process that is in principle quantifiable. And even if 'intense desire' is to be understood as referring to a quantifiable process, the notion of 'just proportion' raises the question as to what would be the criteria for establishing the norm or standard which entitles us to judge the proportion to be 'just'.

By classifying hunger as an appetite, Butler is presumably drawing attention to those well-known facts about the physical or physiological conditions of human survival, that is, that if they wish to survive men need to eat and drink, and if the race is to survive, some men (and women) must gratify their sexual appetites. Thus in the specific case of hunger, to be deprived of food for some considerable time gives rise to the characteristic sensations associated with hunger, and to the concomitant strong desire for food. If one is deprived of food, it is natural to feel hunger and to desire food, and the longer the period of the fast, the more intense the pangs of hunger and the desire for food.

It is also true of human nature that the desire for food to satisfy one's hunger, the gratification of which forms one of the duties to the self, may lead to something else which is morally disapproved of, namely gluttony, an over-indulgence of eating, usually for the sake of the specific pleasure of eating. Perhaps the most plausible construction one can place on the idea of the appetite of hunger rising above its just proportion is that it is meant to mark a distinction between the legitimate desire for food involved in gratifying one's hunger and the morally reprehensible desires of the gluttonous. Likewise the legitimate desire for drink to satisfy thirst can lead to the excesses of the drunkard, whilst the legitimate gratification of the sexual appetite can degenerate into lust. However, it is not at all certain that this is what Butler had in mind. What this examination, I think, makes clear is that the notion of a 'just proportion' when applied to those desires customarily described as appetites is not particularly helpful or illuminating, not at least without a more careful elaboration than is given to it by Butler.

5. *Passions*

In turning to consider Butler's equally sparse references to the passions, let us first note some similarities between what he says about the appetites and what he says about the passions. First, as with the appetites, there are several of them, several 'common particular passions, distinct from benevolence'. Some are such that their 'primary use and intent' is the good of society, others such that their 'primary use and intent' is the good of the self. Again, passions share with appetites the feature that they are 'direct single tendencies toward an object' without distinction of the means of achieving that object; by this, one presumes, Butler means that achieving the object does not involve an intellectual process of deliberation. There is also, as with an appetite, a 'prior suitableness' between a passion and its object. Thus the passion of anger is occasioned by knowing or believing that someone has done me (or those people – or things e.g. property – dear to me) an injury. To say that there is a 'prior suitableness' between anger and injury (the occasion of anger) is no more, presumably, than to say there is an internal relation between the passion and its object. Like the appetites, the passions are 'natural' in that they form part of human nature as God has created it. It would be 'unnatural' to find a man who, on being injured by another, was not angry. Passions are not in themselves a defect of human nature but have been implanted in our constitution by God in order to fulfil some purpose in God's overall design. Reacting angrily to injury from others is part of what is necessary for individual survival, and so in this sense the passion of anger fits into an overall scheme in which God desires, among other things, the survival of human beings. As with the appetites, a particular passion can be gratified without 'being subservient to the particular chief end for which these several principles were respectively in our nature, and if this end, nor any other moral obligation be contradicted, such gratification is innocent'.

There are however differences to be noted between appetites and passions. No appetite can be felt in common, and whilst this is also true of some passions, other passions exist which can be felt in common. Butler's example are shame and resentment. Thus I cannot feel another's hunger nor he mine, but I can share the feeling of humiliation with one who is publicly humiliated. It is also possible for men to indulge a passion in such a way, and to such a degree, that it becomes 'quite another thing from what it originally was in our nature'.

Butler's examples of passions are anger, pride, envy and resentment. The latter is the only one he discusses at length, but as he points out, resentment is not typical of the passions, for it is the only one which has as its object deliberately doing evil or harm to another, and is the only one evil in itself, 'considered in itself very undesirable, what society must very much wish to be without'. Apart from resentment, the passions do not aim at doing evil to others or to the self except when they are 'ungoverned'. As with the appetites, Butler believes there is a natural bound or limit to each passion; to go beyond it is to fall victim to 'ungoverned passion' and this is unnatural.

It is clear from the foregoing that in Butler's usage, the word 'passion' is not interchangeable with 'appetite'. As Duncan-Jones writes, 'hunger, for example, is an appetite, and it would seem incongruous, to Butler as much as to us, to call it a passion; desire of esteem is a passion, and it would seem strange to call it an appetite'.[17] But it is easier to believe there is a distinction between them than to state wherein exactly lies the distinction. Hutcheson offers the suggestion that a passion, 'when it denotes something different from affection . . . is occasioned or attended by some violent bodily motions which keep the mind employed upon the present affair to the exclusion of everything else, and prolongs or strengthens the affection to such a degree that it prevents all deliberate reasoning about conduct'.[18] This would fit Butler's 'ungoverned' passion but cannot be acceptable as a general definition of Butler's use of 'passion'. Elsewhere Hutcheson, who in the preface to the third edition of his *Essay on the Passions*, warmly applauds Butler's *Sermons*, by which he must have been influenced, suggests that 'propensities when they occur without rational desire we may call passions'.[19] Butler however does not attempt to distinguish between a passion and a rational desire. For him both passions and appetites are states of mind which arise naturally in us, granted the appropriate circumstances. In this sense, they both belong to the 'desiring' part of our nature, and not to the 'reasoning', in that they cannot be thought into existence at will. A man whose eyesight is defective cannot see, and he cannot come to see by an act of will or by thinking or believing that he can see. Likewise, a man can only be hungry if he has been deprived of food; apart from this essential condition, he cannot simply will to feel hungry or believe or think that he is feeling hungry. Similarly, a man cannot be angry by simply willing to be angry, or thinking that he is angry or believing that he is angry. Anger arises only if a man knows or believes that certain things are true which occasion his anger. Unless a man knows or believes someone has injured him, where 'injury' represents a wide range of evil which he considers men may have done to him (or indeed that he may have done to himself, for one can be angry at one's own misdeeds as well as at the misdeeds of others) he cannot be, or feel, angry (ignoring for present purposes the distinction between 'feeling angry' and 'being angry'). This is simply to state a conceptual point, namely that there exists an internal relation between 'anger' and its object. Now it is possible to imagine that a man never throughout his life experienced any injury either to himself or to those whom he holds dear. Such a man would not experience, in Butler's terms, the passion of anger. If no one, in his judgement, had injured him or his (including for example his property), such a man could not just will to be angry, or think or believe that he was angry. In order to feel anger, and to be angry, someone must injure us, or we must injure ourselves, and an injury is a quite definite state of affairs that we can specify closely.

What is the main difference between appetites and passions? As Duncan-Jones points out, Butler seems to imply that the object of a passion is something external, and this might be made the ground of the distinction between them, for the object of an appetite is something internal, in the case of the appetites of hunger and thirst, the ingestion of food and drink. But this distinction will not hold, for there appear to be passions whose objects are internal, as for example love of esteem. Perhaps the difference between appetites and passions lies in the different kind or sort of occasion which brings them into existence. An appetite involves a necessary relation between itself and certain determinate physiological states of the body, whereas a passion involves a relation between itself and certain actions of a determinate kind or sort. In the case of anger, this seems to be a relation between holding a belief that some states of affairs are injurious to the self, and those same states of affairs believed to be injurious to the self. The resemblance between an appetite and a passion lies in the fact that in both the relation mentioned comes into existence, granted the concomitant conditions or circumstances, 'naturally'; that is, spontaneously, and not as the result of an intellectual process of reasoning or an act of will on the part of the agent.

6. *Affections*

Most of the characteristic features of the 'passions' belong also to the 'affections'. Affections are states of mind, they are numerous in number, the nature of each 'necessarily implies resting on its object as an end', some of these ends are, according to Butler, related to the public good, and some are related to the good of the individual or private good. As with the passions, an affection 'can rise too high for its just proportion'. On the whole, affections or sentiments motivating actions for the private good are more prevalent than those motivating actions for the public good, and since these affections influence our judgements (judgements presumably about conduct, although Butler does not specifically say so), the private affections are more powerful in their influence on our judgements. Affections, like appetites and passions, are distinct from our reason, although the source of our understanding of the nature of the affections is reason.

If so many features are common to both affections and passions, why did Butler feel the need to refer to them separately? It seems that we can discern some important differences between affections and passions, though unfortunately Butler has not analysed these differences. He does say specifically that affections imply an inward sensation or feeling. He also states that 'the nature of man is so constituted as to feel certain affections upon the sight or contemplation of certain objects'.[20] It is difficult to decide how much emphasis Butler placed here on 'contemplation'. If it means 'reflecting upon the nature and character of the object or action or trait of character', then affections, although being like the passions primarily sentiments or feelings, would seem to be such as can be influenced by reflective reasoning. To this extent the affections would differ from the passions, for at no time does Butler suggest that the reflective element in the nature of man can influence the passions.

The relation between an affection as a 'perception or inward feeling' and the reasoning or reflective element in man's nature is not explicitly discussed by Butler but references to it are made occasionally in the *Sermons*. For example, in his discussion of compassion (Sermon 5) Butler rejects Hobbes's attempt to interpret compassion in terms of fear. In his long note to §1 of this sermon, Butler states that 'real sorrow and concern for the misery of our fellow creatures' is one of the inward feelings or perceptions we experience at the sight of the distress of others. This is properly compassion, an affection 'which directly carries us with calmness and thought to their assistance'.[21] Unfortunately Butler does not explore the precise nature of the relation between discursive thought and an inward feeling or affection which is involved in the process of achieving, through action, the aim or object of an affection.

However, Butler does discuss, in the first of his two sermons on compassion, the general relation between reason and the affections, which, as inward feelings, operate as motives of actions. The context is this. Allowing that compassion motivates actions for the relief of distress, Butler mentions possible objections to conduct motivated by the affection of compassion. One of these is that we should be compassionate 'from reason and duty', and not on the basis of an affection, for are not all passions and affections a weakness, 'what a perfect being must be entirely free from'?[22] Butler's reply to these objections, drawn apparently from Stoic philosophy, is in effect to argue that compassionate action instigated by 'reason alone' is conceivable in a perfect being, but his analysis has to do with imperfect human beings. For human beings, 'reason alone, whatever anyone may wish, is not in reality a sufficient motive of virtue in such a creature as man; but this reason, joined with those affections which God has impressed upon his heart'[23] allows a man to act suitably to his nature.* Earlier in Sermon I Butler has explained that this reason is conscience, 'a principle of reflection in man',[24] who is constituted 'such sort of creature as to reflect on his own nature, his aversions, affections, and passions', and the actions which issue from them. This reflection conjoined to an affection leads to a more settled principle. Butler illustrates this by reference to the affection of parents to their children.

> Thus a parent has the affection of love to his children; this leads him to take care of, to educate, to make due provision for them: the natural affection leads to this; but the reflection that it is his proper business, what belongs to him, that it is right and commendable so to do; this added to the affection becomes a much more settled principle, and carries him on through more labour and difficulties for the sake of his children, than he would undergo from that affection alone, if he thought it, and the course of action it led to, either indifferent or criminal.[25]

Moving from the question of the relation between affection and the reflective element in human nature, we may ask, what are the sorts of things – the 'particular objects', to use Butler's terminology – which excite in us those 'inward sensations' which he calls 'affections'? Instances of what can arouse affections are the actions of others, particular traits of character in others, the settled character of others, and the motives of others – all can arouse affections. And since self-love is an affection, aspects or characteristics of our own personalities can produce affections. In one context Butler states that 'if a man approves of, or hath an affection to, any principle in and for itself . . . it will be the same whether he views it in his own mind, or in another'.[26] 'Principle' here is to be interpreted as a general principle, so that reflection on such can produce an affection.

* Note the similarity to Hume's famous claim that reason is, and ought only to be, the slave of the passions: *Treatise*, Bk II, Part III, Section III.

The quotation is interesting as suggesting that an affection is equivalent to a feeling of approval. Approval in the sense of a deliberate intellectual assessment or judgement belongs of course to conscience and is not an affection. Whether there exists an emotive state of approval to be distinguished from approval as intellectual assessment is quite another question.

Affections, like the passions, are in themselves morally neutral, being the motives of actions on which we pass moral judgements. Affections can be the subject of adverse moral judgements when they rise beyond their just proportion. It is interesting to note however that Butler's list of affections are of sentiments we normally approve of, such as the affection of parents to their children, the affection of love of mankind, reverence, gratitude, trust, tenderness and dependence. On the other hand his examples of passions are of emotions we disapprove of, namely envy, malice, hatred, and pride (in the sense of the 'sin of pride').

In addition to the particular affections, Butler lists the two general affections of self-love and benevolence.[27] We have noted how there exist particular affections whose 'use and intention' is the good of the self, but these are distinct from self-love, which has as its 'use and intention' the general, and not the particular, good of the individual. Similarly there are particular affections which aim at a particular good to others whereas benevolence aims at the general good of others. Every particular affection arises in proportion to one's sense or understanding of the object of the affection. Thus the sight of distress in another arouses compassion, and the strength of the compassion, and of one's compassionate response, depends on one's awareness of the extent of the other person's distress. Each particular affection is thus aroused by a particular 'object' or state of affairs. The general affection of self-love must be aroused by the perception or awareness of the condition of the self as a whole, and the general affection of benevolence must be caused by perception of the state of a certain individual or a group of individuals taken as a whole.

7. *The Status of Benevolence in Butler's Hierarchy*

Mention in the previous paragraph of the general affection of benevolence brings us to one of the questions about benevolence which this discussion of Butler's psychological analysis serves to introduce, namely, what is the status of benevolence in Butler's hierarchy?

Interpreters and commentators on Butler's views have offered divergent answers to this question. Some have claimed that Butler wished to distinguish between self-love and benevolence as rational principles on the one hand and the 'appetites, passions and the affections' as non-rational elements in human nature on the other. Others have argued that self-love alone is to be regarded, apart from conscience, as a rational principle, and is thus superior to benevolence which is to be ranked in the class of 'appetites, passions and affections'. Austin Duncan-Jones falls into the second category. He holds that on Butler's analysis the position assigned to benevolence is uncertain. He writes: 'Butler sometimes speaks as though it occupied a distinct rank, sometimes as though it were merely one of the particular passions. On the whole, his language leans towards representing benevolence as one of the passions, but a passion which calls for special attention for special reasons.'[28] In saying that benevolence is, on the whole, to be regarded as one of the passions, it must be recalled that Duncan-Jones has previously proposed to use 'passions' as a general term for the 'appetites, passions and affections'. According to this suggestion, it would be in order to refer to benevolence as an appetite, for appetites fall as much under the class of 'passions' as the passions proper or the affections. In the light of the foregoing discussion, it is reasonably clear that benevolence can hardly be regarded as an appetite. The choice lies between 'passion' and 'affection'. If it is correct, as has been suggested in our discussion above, that there are some indications for believing that Butler meant to distinguish between 'passions' and 'affections', although in fact he produces no close or sustained discussion of this distinction, it is very likely Butler would have classified benevolence as an affection rather than as a passion. Apart from the frequency of the references to the 'affection of benevolence', the present contention is that by using the expression 'affection of benevolence' Butler meant to convey that benevolence was not a passion. In other words Butler does not in general refer to benevolence as a passion, for he never intended the term 'affection' to be used as a synonym for 'passion'. In support of this we may cite the fact that Butler's list of passions – envy, revenge, malice – are characteristics which we disapprove of, whereas affections are, on the whole, what we approve of. Benevolence clearly falls into the latter category.

In considering this question of the status of benevolence in Butler's analysis, it is important to recall some of his chief aims in undertaking his analysis. One of these was to examine the nature of each element constitutive of human nature as it existed 'in itself', and another was to ask what relation each element bore to the other elements in human nature. These two questions can be asked of Butler's discussion of benevolence: what did he think it was in itself? and secondly, how is it related to the other elements which make up the system or constitution of human nature?

Those who follow Duncan-Jones in believing that Butler is not very clear about the status to be accorded to benevolence in his hierarchy are, in general, quite adamant that he assigned to self-love – or cool, reasonable self-love – a status or position in the hierarchy quite separate and distinct from that assigned to the class of 'appetites, passions and affections'. It is possible therefore to ask what are the criteria used by Butler for distinguishing self-love so sharply from the appetites, passions and affections. It is further possible to ask whether benevolence, according to Butler's analysis of it, resembles self-love by satisfying the same criteria which distinguish self-love from the appetites, passions, and affections.

By examining closely what he says about self-love, we can set out Butler's reasons for assigning a 'superior' status to self-love in his hierarchy, over the appetites, passions and affections. First, self-love is said to be a 'principle', in the sense of something which moves or motivates an agent to act. No great stress need be placed on this factor, for in the same sense, the appetites, passions and affections are principles of our nature. More relevantly, self-love is said to be an affection, but one that differs from the several particular affections in that it is a 'general affection'. Significantly, Butler never refers to self-love as either a passion or an appetite, but there are numerous references to its being an affection. Self-love can be overcome by passion or appetite,[29] and the passions 'have absolutely no bound or measure but that which is set by self-love or moral considerations'.[30] The question that arises is, what is the difference between a particular and a general affection? The difference lies in the nature of their respective 'objects'. The 'object' of a particular affection is particular, that is, the object or aim or end of the affection of compassion is to relieve distress in the person (or persons) suffering it. If there are no instances of persons suffering distress, interpreted widely to include any kind of physical or mental distress, then it is not possible for anyone to feel compassion or be compassionate. (Here again it is necessary to ignore the distinction between 'feeling compassion' and 'being compassionate'.) When we say that the object of compassion is to relieve distress, we are being relatively specific, in the sense that we recognise the specific aim of compassion, which is to relieve distress. Of course it is possible to insist at this point that to say that the object of compassion is the relief of distress is no more than to make a conceptual point, and that the real difficulty, which may well involve differences in moral view-points or convictions, arises when one tries to specify more precisely what is to count as 'distress'. Presumably everyone would agree that the suffering inflicted on innocent victims by an earthquake is certainly the kind of distress which it is the legitimate aim of compassion to relieve, but not everyone would agree that the suffering now experienced by one who has ruined his health and his estates by gratifying his unruly desires inevitably counts as distress to be relieved by another's compassion. And even in the case of earthquake victims, if one firmly believed that the earthquake was evidence of God's wrath being visited upon the sins of men, one might not believe that their suffering was a proper object of one's compassion.

To say that 'distress' is the object of compassion is to be relatively specific by drawing attention to a description of a determinate state of affairs. It could easily be the case, contingently, that no one was actually experiencing distress, and we would understand what was meant by saying 'no one is in distress'. However, the object of self-love is said to be 'a general desire to the happiness of the self', or in contemporary idiom, 'the long-term interest of the self'. Now both of these expressions are less specific than the object of an affection such as compassion, which is the relief of distress, in that no precise description of the state of affairs answering to the long-term interest of the self or the happiness of the self can be given. This is, I think, what Butler had in mind by saying that the object of self-love is general, whereas the object of every particular affection is particular. Whether he was correct in implying that 'the happiness of the self' or 'the long term interest of the self' is less specific and more open-ended than 'relief of distress' as the object of compassion is another question.

Self-love cannot operate in a vacuum, and in this consideration lies Butler's third criterion: self-love is a second-order affection in the sense that unless the 'appetites, passions and affections' existed, it would not be possible for anyone to seek the long-term interest of the self. Unless affections exist which aim at realising particular states of affairs believed to be good for the self, it would not be possible to organise them into a harmonious system in which their fulfilment contributes to the long-term good or happiness of the self.

Finally, perhaps the most important criterion which distinguishes self-love from 'the particular affections' is that it seems 'inseparable from all sensible creatures, who can reflect upon themselves and their own interest or happiness, so as to have that interest an object to their minds: . . . [it] belongs to man as a reasonable creature reflecting upon his own interest or happiness. The other [affections] are quite distinct from reason.'[31] The crucial consideration introduced in this criterion is the reference to the fact that the object of self-love, whatever it may be (and Butler suggests it is 'the general happiness of the self'), is something discovered by 'reflection', that is by an intellectual process of considering what is in the self's long-term interest, whereas a particular affection is something whose object is not so produced by reason, though of course we require reason for its recognition. Our nature is so constituted that when, for example, one sees another person in distress, the feeling or affection of compassion naturally arises in one (if it does not, one is unnatural). Once compassion has arisen, its object, i.e. relief of distress, is immediately apparent.

It seems clear, therefore, that having its object produced or thought out by the reflective or reasoning element in man's nature constitutes, on Butler's view, a crucial difference, so far as self-love is concerned, between this general affection and all the other particular affections, although Butler in fact says very little about the way in which reason functions in its reflective or intellectual capacity. Even so, he says one important thing about it in the context of his discussion of self-love. As a constitutive element in human nature whose 'object' is outlined by reason, self-love belongs 'inseparably' to human nature. Presumably this statement implies that we could conceive human nature lacking some of the affections it now possesses. For example, we can imagine a world in which human beings lacked compassion but not filial or paternal affection. Lacking compassion whilst possessing the other affections would not mean that they were no longer human. But if we conceive of beings who possess all human affections but lack self-love, that is the notion, produced by reason, of these human affections harmonised in the long-term interest of the self, such beings would not be 'human'. It belongs, according to Butler, to the nature of human beings that they are both rational and moral. Cool or reasonable self-love is an essential constituent both of their rational and of their moral nature.

In the light of this review of Butler's criteria for self-love, let us now consider whether what he says about benevolence satisfies the same criteria for what it is for something to be a 'general affection'.

First, benevolence is said to be a 'principle' in exactly the same sense as all the appetites, passions and affections are motivating principles. It is also a 'natural' principle, like cool or reasonable self-love. Moreover it is an affection; 'if there be any affection in human nature,' writes Butler, 'the object and end of which is the good of another, this is itself benevolence',[32] '[benevolence] is an affection to the good of our fellow-creatures'.[33] The object of benevolence is general: it is a 'general affection'.[34] If it is possible to call self-love a second-order affection, so it is benevolence. Compassion is an affection to the good of others but it is particular in that it is directed towards those in distress. Paternal affection is also an affection to the good of others but is particular in being directed to the good of our children. Filial affection is an affection to the good of others but is particular in being directed to the good of our parents. The general affection of benevolence stands in the same relation to those particular affections as self-love does towards that group of affections having as their end the good of the self.

How far is it possible to extend the scope of benevolence? Butler seems quite firm in believing that the number of individuals who can be the object of any one man's benevolence is strictly limited; 'the universe', he says, 'should [not] be the object of benevolence to such creatures as we are;'[35] mankind is too general an object for benevolence. Incidentally this quotation reinforces the present contention that the point of qualifying the name of an affection with the adjective 'general' is to draw attention to the nature of its object. Thus love of neighbour, 'that part of mankind which comes under our immediate notice' is 'less general'[36] in its reference than benevolence, but even the reference of benevolence is not so general as to comprise absolutely everyone that exists in the world.

One difference between a 'general' and a 'particular' affection lies in the temporal aspect of the respective objects of the affections. The object of a particular affection (for example relieving the distressed, which is the object of compassion) may exist for only a short temporal period, for there is no longer any need to relieve distress when it has been relieved. But the object of self-love – the true interest of the self – persists as long as the self exists. Similarly, so long as other individuals exist, there is an object for one's benevolence as long as one lives.

In discussing self-love above,[37] it was suggested that one of the important features which distinguished self-love from the other self-regarding affections was the fact that it was a 'rational principle' in the sense of having its object formed by reason. Can this also be said of benevolence? The answer seems to be in the affirmative. As in the case of self-love, Butler gives only one or two references to the relation between the reasoning or reflective element and benevolence, but these are revealing. In discussing compassion Butler refers to 'a settled reasonable principle of benevolence'.[38] But more significantly he asserts that when benevolence is spoken of as the sum of virtue, 'it is not spoken of as a blind propension, but as a principle in reasonable creatures, and so to be directed by their reason. . . . That will lead us to consider distant consequences as well as the immediate tendency of an action.'[39] Benevolence, like self-love, is to be distinguished from the particular affections in that the idea of the object of this 'general affection' is formulated by reason. A brief indication is given here by Butler as to how reason arrives at the idea of the object of benevolence in a particular set of circumstances, namely by considering the 'distant consequences' as well as the 'immediate tendency' of the contemplated action.

The conclusion which this examination of Butler's analysis of self-love and benevolence would seem to suggest is that, with regard to his account of the nature of self-love and benevolence, there is no substantial difference between them. Both are 'affections' and both are intimately related to the reasoning or reflective element in human nature, in that the 'objects' of both are formulated by reason, that is, by an intellectual process of reasoning, although Butler says little about its nature.

The claim that benevolence is a *general* affection like self-love, based as it is on Butler's explicit statement to this effect in the second sermon, 'Upon the Love of our Neighbour' (Sermon 12), viz. 'the proportion which the two general affections, benevolence and self-love, bear to each other' cannot be allowed to go unchallenged. The reason for this is that in the previous sermon, 'On the Love of our Neighbour' (Sermon 11), Butler includes several references[40] which unmistakably imply that benevolence is a particular and not a general affection. What are we to make of this evidence? These apparently contradictory views about benevolence certainly account for the disagreement amongst commentators in interpreting Butler on benevolence. For example, Duncan-Jones typifies the school which believes that benevolence is no more than one of the passions (or affections), though one that indeed demands special consideration. Traditional interpreters such as C. D. Broad and A. E. Taylor argue that benevolence shares with self-love the status of a 'rational principle' and so is not to be equated with the class of 'appetites, passions and affections'. Disagreement amongst the critics does not unfortunately help us to resolve the problem posed by Butler's seemingly inconsistent statements. One possibility is of course to admit Butler's inconsistency, on the grounds that perfect consistency cannot be reasonably expected in a collection of occasional sermons. Another solution is to point out that Sermon 11, where the stress on benevolence as a particular affection appears, is in fact dealing with the *particular affection* of the love of neighbour which is to be distinguished from the general affection of benevolence, even though Butler carelessly in this sermon refers frequently to the particular affection of love of neighbour as benevolence. Those who are reluctant to level a charge of inconsistency against so careful a writer as Butler may find comfort in this latter suggestion.

The thesis that self-love and benevolence are a sub-class of affections, to be separately identified within the larger class of affections, can be further supported by two more general considerations. First, in the Preface, written for the second edition of the *Sermons*, in order to summarise the drift of his main arguments, Butler repeatedly affirms that his aim is to set out the elements constitutive of human nature, that is, 'the appetites, passions, and affections and the principle of reflection'.[41] By '*the* principle of reflection' Butler clearly means to refer to conscience, which he singles out by using the definite description. Distinguishing the 'appetites, passions and affections' on the one hand, and *the* principle of reflection on the other, implies a two-tier analysis of the elements in human nature, a division between the emotive or feeling elements on the one hand, and the reasoning, deliberative and intellectual element on the other. On this analysis, self-love and benevolence, being affections or feelings, belong decidedly to the emotive side of human nature. Had Butler intended a tripartite analysis, as is implied by Broad's category of rational principles, to include self-love and benevolence, he could reasonably be expected to have made this clear in his second edition preface, but he does not, and in this context, the omission is significant.

Secondly, if we examine Butler's remarks about conscience we gain a firm impression that for Butler the superiority of conscience lies precisely in its unique character as a constituent of human nature. Butler emphasises that conscience is the *one* superior principle of reflection,[42] whose office is 'to adjust, manage, and preside over' the varying elements in human nature.[43] It is essentially 'the superior principle of reflection', superior precisely because it alone approves or disapproves the external actions or the internal motives of human beings, 'pronounces determinately some actions to be in themselves just, right, good;'[44] and by virtue of this faculty is man a moral agent, a law unto himself. Conscience then is 'a particular kind of reflection'[45] which possesses that '*natural supremacy* of the faculty which surveys, approves or disapproves the several affections',[46] including, of course, the affections of self-love and benevolence. There is no suggestion that in relation to conscience, self-love and benevolence are anything more than affections which conscience surveys and approves. Admittedly, in discussing conscience, Butler considers its relation to self-love, as in discussing self-love he had occasion to refer to conscience. He states: 'conscience and self-love, if we understand our true happiness, always lead us the same way.'[47] But we must remember that in his general analysis of human nature Butler is very much concerned to counter a view very popular in some eighteenth-century circles, namely that the life of virtue must of its nature be incompatible with the aims of self-love. Butler opposes this view by insisting that the aims of cool, reasonable self-love, if properly understood, are perfectly coincident with the deliverances of conscience. Yet another view prominent in the eighteenth century, reflected for example in Hutcheson's writings,[48] was that benevolence and virtue are coincident. Butler shares this view, as when he writes, 'benevolence seems in the strictest sense to include in it all that is good and worthy'.[49] This is why he does not feel it necessary to make any special mention of the relation between conscience and benevolence, as he does of the relation between conscience and self-love.

Self-love and benevolence are both 'affections', though affections which demand special consideration. If we ask Butler's second question, what is the relation of each to the other elements in human nature, we find that the answer is not the same for both. Conscience is certainly superior in authority, on Butler's analysis, to all the other elements, superior over both self-love and benevolence. However, next to conscience comes self-love which is superior to all the other elements, including the affection of benevolence.[50] In this sense, benevolence is one of the affections which in real human nature is governed by and is subordinate to self-love. To the extent, if it is possible, that we can give meaning to the notion of superior and inferior elements in human nature, to that extent there is a difference in status between self-love and benevolence, but a difference that does not obliterate the fact that both belong to the feeling or 'affection' side of human nature.

8. *Butler's Analysis of Benevolence*

In the last section the status assigned to benevolence in Butler's hierarchy was discussed. In this section the aim is to consider what he has to say positively about benevolence itself. In order to follow, and appreciate, Butler's thought on benevolence, it is necessary to examine what he says about benevolence as an affection, whether particular or not; that is, as a motivating force which leads men to act benevolently. As was stated earlier, Butler was, in common with many thinkers of his age, particularly preoccupied with the attempt to give a psychological account, in terms of one powerful motive overcoming another, of the genesis of action in general, and of moral action in particular. In this respect, benevolence is a motive which accounts for men acting in certain determinate ways. Butler also stressed that men possessed reason; and indeed this reason, under the guise of conscience, plays a vital role in his analysis of the psychology of moral action. But reason also enables us to form general notions or ideas of things. Thus, apart from benevolence as a motive, which we recognise by means of our reason, we possess a notion or idea, or in modern philosophical terminology, a concept of benevolence. In this section we must examine what Butler has to say about benevolence regarded as a motive, and what he says about the concept of benevolence.

Benevolence identified as a motive of action is defined variously as 'an affection to the good of our fellow creatures', 'love of neighbour', and 'good-will'. As was suggested above, the nature of the 'object' of this affection is general. Butler's definition of the love of neighbour gives us the best indication of what he thought its object was. Love of neighbour is directed to 'that part of the universe, that part of mankind, that part of our country, which comes under our immediate notice, acquaintance, and influence, and with which we have to do'.[51] This definition applies to the common men, who do not 'consider their affections as affecting the whole community of which they are members'.[52] The 'upper part', i.e. the ruling class, can exercise a 'uniform love' of their country, but as kingdoms and governments are large, this is more than can be expected of the ordinary person. As for love of the whole universe, this can only be predicated of a perfect being. As this love is directed towards the happiness of the creator, the perfection of God's goodness lies in his love of the entire universe.

Having answered the question to whom is love of neighbour directed, we may now ask, to *what* is it directed? It is directed to the 'good of our neighbour'. Negatively, this will prevent us doing him injury; positively, it will lead us to promote his good, that is, to take care of his interests, joys and sorrows, to regard them as our own, which is to 'consider ourselves as having a real share in his happiness'.[53] As self-love makes us particularly sensitive to instances of humanity, justice or injustice exercised towards ourselves, so love of neighbour makes us sensitive to instances of humanity, justice or injustice exercised towards our neighbour.[54] As the object of self-love is the interest of the self, so the object of benevolence is the interest of others. Interest or the good of the self Butler identifies with happiness and the absence of misery. Likewise, in working for the good of my neighbour I seek, by my actions, his happiness and freedom from misery.

Butler understands by happiness 'the enjoyment of those objects which are by nature adapted to our several faculties. These particular enjoyments make up the sum total of our happiness.'[55] The satisfaction of our legitimate desires (that is, in Butler's language, of the appetites, passions and affections) each in due degree, is what constitutes happiness. This satisfaction brings or is attended by pleasure or enjoyment, but Butler does not equate this pleasure, as Mill tends to do, with happiness. Pleasurable sensations are not the sole ingredient of happiness for Butler but the natural satisfaction of the natural impulses we possess. Indeed to seek deliberately the sensation of pleasure may prevent us from realising the satisfaction of our natural impulses, i.e. appetites, passions and affections in due degree, and this causes unhappiness.

It is commonly held that the desires whose satisfaction most brings happiness are those for 'riches, honours and the gratification of sensual appetites'.[56] But Butler points out that the fulfilment of the desire to seek the happiness of others is for some what is most deeply satisfying, and they adopt this as 'the end of their life'. Indeed, fulfilment of the desire to seek the happiness of our neighbour brings not only that satisfaction which we experience when we successfully fulfil or satisfy a desire but also the realisation that the aim of the desire is virtuous. 'Love of neighbour, considered as a *virtuous principle*, is gratified by a consciousness of endeavouring to promote the good of others, but considered as a natural affection, its gratification consists in the actual accomplishment of this endeavour.'[57]

Butler discusses at length in the first of his two sermons 'Upon the Love of our Neighbour' (Sermon 11) the relation between self-love and benevolence. It is commonly believed, he states, that they are incompatible, their 'objects' or aims and ends necessarily opposed. He argues effectively against this contention. He argues that benevolence and self-love are 'perfectly coincident'. How can this be so? We can readily understand how unreasonable self-love or selfishness conflicts with benevolence. Unreasonable self-love or undue selfishness always leads me to act for my own gain or benefit, and I am diverted from acting for the good of others. The object of cool or reasonable self-love is however that state of affairs called 'the good of the self' by Butler, which he is inclined to identify with the self's happiness. How then can what is for the happiness of the self coincide with acting for the good (=happiness) of others? According to Butler, the link between them is to be discovered in the fact that acting for the good of others is what gives a man most satisfaction – 'the greatest satisfactions to ourselves depend upon our having benevolence in a due degree',[58] '. . . in one respect benevolence contributes more to private interest, i.e. enjoyment, than any other of the particular common affections.' If the object of self-love is the happiness of the self, conceived of as a state of deep satisfaction, then self-love and benevolence need not, and are not, in conflict, for nothing more promotes the 'deep satisfaction' which is the aim of the self-love than 'benevolence to a due degree', or 'real benevolence' as Butler also calls it. 'Whoever will consider all the possible respects and relations which any particular affection can have to self-love and private interest, will, I think, see demonstrably, that benevolence is not in any respect more at variance with self-love, than any other particular affection whatever, but that it is in every respect, at least, as friendly to it.'[59] The main difference between self-love and benevolence is that every action motivated by self-love is necessarily 'interested', that is, aimed at the interest or good of the self, whereas an action motivated by benevolence may or may not be interested. This is true of every other motive except self-love.

'Benevolence is no more disinterested than any of the common particular passions' (where 'passions' here refers without distinction to the class of 'appetites, passions, and affections'). This is another of Butler's contentions. Here we must distinguish between the object of an affection, that is, the particular state of affairs brought into existence when that object is achieved, and the fact that every affection is the agent's, that is, is *his* desire, belongs as an item in his consciousness or in his autobiography. Affections (as indeed do passions and appetites in this respect) possess different objects, but all my affections are alike in this respect, they are *my* affections. In this benevolence is on a par with any other affection whatsoever, and is no more 'disinterested' than some other particular affection. Achieving the object of my benevolence gives me satisfaction as does achieving the object of my self-regarding affections or desires. Thus my successfully relieving the distress of another gives me satisfaction although the aim or object of my action was to relieve his distress, something which does not directly benefit me.

Hitherto we have discussed Butler's view on benevolence in relation to benevolence or love of neighbour when regarded as a motive inspiring a particular course of action, that is, one believed to aim at the good of another. In addition to discussing benevolence as an affection or feeling which motivates action, Butler also considers briefly the notion of a benevolent man or character, one in which benevolence is a settled principle or disposition of character.

The characteristics of a benevolent disposition are unmistakable: they are meekness, easiness of temper, a readiness to forgo our rights for the sake of peace, freedom from mistrust, and a disposition to believe well of our neighbour. All these are said to accompany love and good-will to our neighbour.[60] Needless to say, Butler offers no analysis of a disposition, nor does he more than mention these characteristic qualities of the benevolent disposition.

He does however elaborate on two further points. He says something about the way in which the disposition is formed, and he offers some observations on how we can judge whether a person is benevolent or not.

In considering the question, how is it that the benevolent man possesses all the virtues?,[61] Butler explains that when it is claimed that benevolence is the sum of virtue we are not referring to benevolence simply as a feeling or affection, but to this particular feeling as amenable to reason, 'directed by reason'. As such, 'it will lead us to consider distant consequences, as well as the immediate tendency of an action; . . . reason, considered merely as subservient to benevolence, as assisting to produce the greater good, will teach us to have particular regard to those relations [i.e. obligations to families, children, friends, neighbours].[62] Thus benevolence includes in it the sum of all virtues when, in striving to achieve the good of others, it is guided by reason, thus forming a 'settled reasonable principle of benevolence' in a man.

In this notion of reason influencing benevolence, Butler uses figurative language which raises questions he leaves unanswered. It affords however an interesting glimpse of his undeveloped, or at least unstated, thoughts about the way in which rational reflection enters into the description and explanation of moral actions. Butler is not content with descriptions of moral actions couched exclusively in terms of the 'natural affections'.

To turn to the matter of assessing whether another man is a benevolent man or not, Butler argues that such a judgement does not rest solely on attempting to assess the strength of the benevolent motive which caused a particular action. In order to judge a man benevolent, it is not sufficient to establish that he acted benevolently, in the sense of seeking another's good or happiness intentionally, and not accidentally or inadvertently, but one must attempt to establish the strength of the benevolent motive in relation to other motives existing in his mind, in particular its relation to self-love. Thus, 'the influence which benevolence has upon our actions, and how far it goes toward forming our character, is not determined by the degree itself of this principle in our mind; but by the proportion it has to self-love and other principles.'[63]

In fact, we cannot directly assess the strength of a particular motive, or 'the proportion' that holds between it and any other motive. Our only method of assessment is indirect, by considering actions and deciding from what motive they issue. Butler does not indicate how we can discover in actions the motives from which they spring. However, in so far as common-sense talk contains frequent references to strong and powerful desires or motives, Butler makes a valid point in suggesting that judging the benevolence of a benevolent man requires that we must have due regard to the strength of his benevolent motive in relation to his other existing motives. This is however figurative language, even if used by common sense, and the philosophical difficulty lies in giving it an analysis which is both meaningful and precise. Butler does in fact suggest that each man must decide for himself what is the due proportion or relation between self-love and benevolence, and that this will vary with each man's differing circumstances. He contends that one man cannot decide for another what it ought to be – 'how ridiculous soever it would be, for any to attempt to determine it for another'.[64]

From the discussion of benevolence as a motive, and benevolence as a settled disposition of character, I turn to remarks in Butler's *Sermons* which can be construed as suggesting an outline, however inadequate, of a concept of benevolence.

We have seen how 'love of neighbour' or 'an affection to the good of our fellow creatures' are expressions which name that affection or feeling in human beings which motivates actions directed towards the happiness of our fellow creatures. But according to Butler, there exist other affections in human nature whose end or object is the good of others. These are the affections of friendship and of compassion, and paternal and filial affections. That is to say, instances of compassionate actions, of actions expressing filial or paternal affection, are also instances of benevolence, being included in the idea of doing good to others, an idea formulated by reason, though Butler does not explain how reason forms it. These are examples of benevolence in addition to those benevolent actions which are motivated directly by the benevolent affection strictly, namely love of neighbour.

Of these further instances of benevolence, Butler provides a detailed analysis of only one, compassion; in this he goes a step further than Hutcheson, who mentions, but without further enquiry, the connection between benevolence and compassion.

As Butler's analysis of compassion may throw light on our understanding of benevolence, some features of it may be briefly noticed. In his analysis of compassion Butler maintains that the object of this affection is the relief of those in misery or distress. Thus the sight of persons known or believed to be in distress arouses three distinct perceptions or feelings:[65]

(*a*) real sorrow or concern for the misery of our fellow creatures;
(*b*) some degree of satisfaction in us from a consciousness of freedom from that misery;
(*c*) it is not unnatural to reflect upon our own liableness to the same and other calamities.

Of these, (*a*) only is properly compassion although (*b*) and (*c*) frequently accompany it, and the object of the feeling or affection is a person or persons in distress, which 'directly carries us with calmness and thought to their assistance'. Butler concedes that the sight of those in distress may not arouse the feeling of 'real sorrow or concern', but may be the occasion or cause of one or both of the other perceptions. The sight of those in distress is thus a necessary but not a sufficient condition of compassion. The sufficient condition is the real sorrow or concern for the person (or persons) in distress. Butler does not say a great deal about this factor of felt sorrow or concern, except to counter Hobbes's attempt to explain away compassion and pity by claiming that compassion is no more than the fear we feel for our own safety at the sight of distress to others. The latter is roughly equivalent to element (*c*) in Butler's analysis, and so his argument against Hobbes is that he has mistaken one possible element in compassion for the whole of it. Butler contends that if compassion were reduced to the fear for our own safety aroused by the sight of others in distress, this would be due to some kind of mutual sympathy, something very different from what Hobbes in fact had in mind, something which would not be an example of 'our substituting others for ourselves, but it would be an example of our substituting ourselves for others. And as it would not be an instance of benevolence, so neither would it be any instance of self-love.'[66]

Butler concludes that compassion, because of the frequency of its occurrence in human beings, is 'an original distinct particular affection'. It is in fact felt more frequently than the feeling of rejoicing at the prosperity of others. Butler's explanation of this is that it reflects a truth about our human nature and the circumstances of the world in which we find ourselves. The prosperous and successful do not need our help whereas those in distress do require our aid, hence our nature has been so created as to make us feel compassion more often than we are able to rejoice at the success of others. The very existence of compassion in us towards the distressed in turn gives hope and encouragement to those in distress that they are not being abandoned to their fate by their fellow beings. Without this knowledge that others care for them, the misery of the distressed would be greater than in fact it is.

Butler also deals with the Stoic argument that it is a weakness in human beings to have any kind of feelings, and in particular, to feel compassion for others. Butler argues that this Stoic contention could only be upheld if we thought it wise to get rid of all feelings and affections. According to Butler, this is not possible for these affections are part and parcel of human nature. God may possess a nature which lacks feeling or affections, but God's nature is perfect, and its perfection is not for human beings. Moreover the argument which denies the existence of compassion presupposes that man can act benevolently towards his fellow creatures on the basis of rational calculations alone. Butler's position on this point is similar to Hume's, as has already been noticed. Reason can tell us what we should do if we are to act compassionately or benevolently, but for Butler the deliverances of reason are not a sufficient motive for action in such a creation as man: feelings or affections are required to motivate his actions. Butler shrewdly notes that those who support the Stoics in advocating that the feelings, especially the charitable feelings such as compassion, should be eradicated from man's nature, are in fact more successful in smothering these charitable feelings than they are in suppressing their powerful passions of envy, pride and resentment. Moreover they fail to acknowledge the well-known psychological fact that those who are hard-hearted and lack fellow-feeling towards their fellows are persons grown coarse and callous, who are 'insensible to most other satisfactions but those of the grossest kinds'.[67] Or again, men of pleasure are hard of heart because they wish to pursue their pleasures: but they are very sensitive to envy and pride.[68]

The first sermon on Compassion (Sermon 5) concludes on the note that no one can reasonably deny the existence of the simple feeling of compassion in the generality of mankind. Whoever does not feel this natural affection is in some sense unnatural, and only a highly sophisticated philosophy, such as that of Hobbes, trying to be too clever by half, would seek to argue the absurdity that compassion is not a real feeling.

Butler's second sermon on Compassion (Sermon 6) does not add a great deal to his analysis. He makes the point that compassion has the negative role of restraining the passions of envy and resentment, whose objects tend to lie in the misery of others, as well as the positive task of removing the distress of others.

Another new point he makes is that it is much more in our power to relieve the distress of others, though of course it is not always in our power to do so, than it is to act positively to increase the happiness of others; not again that it is never in our power to act positively to increase the happiness of others, but the occasions are fewer. In this sense, benevolence in us is weak. It is also weak in that it is directly in competition with our own powerful selfish interests, which frequently overcome such feelings of benevolence as we possess. The sight of the distress of others, however, rarely fails to arouse us to act for the sake of others, and so compassion is a powerful reinforcement of what would otherwise be weak and impotent feelings of benevolence. Here Butler distinguishes quite clearly between the affection or feeling of benevolence, and the affection or feeling of compassion.

One of Butler's cardinal assumptions throughout his analysis of human nature is that 'every affection, as distinct from a principle of reason, may rise too high and be beyond its just proportion'.[69] Compassion is no exception. It is possible therefore for a man to feel more sorrow for the distress of another 'than belongs to his share'. Butler does not elaborate on this notion nor does he suggest the criteria for recognising a situation in which a man feels more distress for another than is warranted. But he clearly implies that because a man may overreact to the distress of one person, he may then be prevented – that is, presumably, lack the necessary resources, both material and otherwise – from helping another in distress who stands more genuinely in need of his help. Although this is a very real possibility, our common observation of the actions of men suggests, argues Butler, that there is far more danger of a lack of compassion than too much of it. Accordingly those general rules which are formulated as a guide to the moral life should be biased in favour of encouraging and stimulating compassion.

What Butler says about the danger of feeling too much compassion applies equally to the feeling or affection of benevolence, 'which may rise too high and be beyond its just proportion'. If we respond to some situations by feeling too much benevolence, we may later lack adequate resources to help those genuinely in need of our benevolent attentions. The danger however is slight. Human beings are so prone to acting selfishly that men feel too little, not too much, benevolence.

Neither in the case of the affection of compassion nor the affection of benevolence does Butler explain why it is that the affection is felt more strongly 'than belongs to one's share'. He hints that it is the function of reason to gauge the right degree of response, but suggests that feelings can become so strong that a man is prompted to act in a way contrary to the dictates of reason. At this point there should enter considerations of a man's capacities and abilities, but Butler does not explore the matter. For instance, some obviously possess greater intellectual ability than others, and so are better able to assess intellectually what action is required in a particular set of circumstances. Some men presumably know what is the correct response to a given set of circumstances and others simply do not know this. But even some of those who know fail to act in accord with their knowledge. They act on a felt emotion more strongly 'than belongs to their share'. This would be described, as it is in certain legal cases, as acting on 'irresistible impulse'. But this raises doubts whether impulses are ever irresistible, and if they are, does this indicate a lack of some capacity or other? Or again, by what criteria does one distinguish between a man who acted on 'irresistible impulse' but who is judged normally to possess the strength of will to control such impulses, and another who acts on irresistible impulse because he is so weak-willed that he can never resist his impulses? These are questions Butler does not discuss.

Nor again does he discuss the quite different case of a man who recognises, and thereby understands, a situation of distress in another, but responds to this situation not by feeling compassion but by feeling one of the other two possible affections which may, according to Butler, accompany the feeling of compassion, but are not to be mistaken for it. These are the feeling of satisfaction that one is not oneself caught up in the disaster, and the feeling that one might have been so easily involved in this same, or similar, disaster. Presumably there are, contingently, cases where a man who does not feel compassion possesses both the intellectual ability to assess the right degree of compassionate response to a particular example of a distress, and the capacity to act compassionately in a manner and to a degree appropriate to the circumstances. Why is it that such a man does not feel compassion? Butler definitely suggests such a man is 'unnatural', to the extent that he lacks the feeling of compassion. If it is true that feeling compassion is natural to human beings, failure to feel compassion on a particular occasion, in the case of a man who otherwise is judged to possess the necessary capacities and abilities which enable a person to act compassionately, can only be explained, as Butler suggests, in terms of more powerful selfish feelings which overcome the compassionate impulses. And if a man consistently fails to respond compassionately in the appropriate circumstances, then the capacity to feel compassion will become atrophied, and will wither away. Thereby a man acquires a dispositional trait not to feel compassion; he becomes hard-hearted and this is 'unnatural', on Butler's analysis.

But we can very easily imagine an example that raises a difficulty for Butler's view. It is logically conceivable that, if the capacity to feel compassion is 'natural' to human beings, there exists, contingently, a person who cannot (empirically) feel compassion because he was born that way: in other words, the capacity to feel compassion has not been inherited, and the lack is not due to the decay and decline of a capacity he once originally possessed. In such a case, the inability to feel compassion would resemble the inability, which is a very distressing phenomenon, of some mothers to feel motherly affection for their young babies.

Now if such a case existed, Butler's generalisation 'all men naturally feel compassion except where the capacity has been allowed to degenerate and disappear' ceases to be valid. This immediately raises the question of the logical status of Butler's claim, 'all men naturally feel compassion'. Butler can advance it as a conceptual claim: a man who has never been able to feel compassion is not strictly or fully a man; and a man who once was able to feel compassion but has allowed this capacity to degenerate is 'unnatural'. Alternatively, Butler can be understood as making a moral and not a conceptual point. Basic to his moral view of the world, and of man's place in it as God's creature, is that a man, when he is able, should respond compassionately to instances of distress and misery in others.

This discussion of Butler's treatment of the affection or feeling of compassion can profitably be used to illuminate his much briefer references to the affection or feeling of benevolence.

All men, according to Butler, possess naturally the capacity to feel benevolence towards their fellow beings, and the aim or object of this feeling can be described as 'a general desire for their good or happiness'. A man who does not experience this benevolent feeling is 'unnatural', and this unnatural state of affairs has arisen because he has allowed other self-regarding feelings to dominate and conquer his benevolent affections. As with compassion Butler does not countenance the possibility of a man being born into this world lacking the capacity to feel benevolence. Unlike compassion, the state of affairs which causes or brings the feeling of benevolence into existence, as the sight of distress in others arouses compassion, cannot be specified positively, in the way that 'distress' specifies that to which compassion is a response. Negatively, it can be stated that all states of affairs involving our fellows are states of affairs which do not preclude the possibility of one being able to respond benevolently to them, except for those cases where the other person (or persons) has acted maliciously or harmfully towards oneself, in which case the appropriate response may not be a benevolent one. The very general nature of the 'object' of benevolence means that the opportunities for acting benevolently are far more numerous than those for acting compassionately. The very frequency of such opportunities also means that failure to act benevolently is much more frequent, because of the competing claims of self-regarding impulses, than is failure to act compassionately. Hence benevolence is 'weak' in the generality of men, according to Butler: not that men do not feel benevolence, but they fail to act on it. Hence an increase in the welfare and happiness of mankind requires more, not less, benevolence.

What was said about capacities and abilities in relation to compassion applies also to the affection of benevolence. It is possible for a man to feel benevolence to a degree greater than is warranted by the circumstances of a particular case, and so a man may feel benevolently more strongly than is 'his due share'. As with compassion, the danger of this is slight, and general moral rules should be biased in favour of encouraging and developing benevolence, even though there is a possible and undeniable risk that some may act more benevolently than they should.

Acting more benevolently in a particular set of circumstances – again Butler does not discuss the criteria by which one decides what is the correct benevolent response in a particular

situation – can, like the similar case of over-reacting compassionately, have two unfortunate consequences: as a result
of such action, one may lack the resources to act benevolently
in another subsequent case, which is more deserving; or one
may have dissipated so much of one's resources that a sufficient
balance, appropriate and necessary for the needs of one's own
welfare, no longer exists. If the rich man literally obeyed
Christ's command to go and sell all he possessed and give to
the poor, this would be both unwise and unnatural, on Butler's
analysis, being a clear case of the affection of benevolence
'rising too high and beyond its just proportion'.

The capacities and abilities implied by Butler's notion of acting on a benevolent affection are, as with compassion, the
ability to assess the due degree of benevolent action required
in a particular situation, and the capacity to act on this affection, not allowing other competing affections to override or
stifle it. The physical and mental capacities implied in all
deliberate action (that is, the capacity to intend a particular
action, and the capacity physically to initiate the necessary
changes in states of affairs, which we normally call 'actions')
are presupposed by the notion of acting on a benevolent
affection.

As with compassion, it is important to ask what is the logical
status of Butler's claim that 'all men naturally feel benevolence'.
It is either a conceptual claim or a moral claim. If a conceptual claim, it entails that a person who cannot feel the affection of benevolence is not in some sense fully a moral being.
Alternatively it can be regarded as a moral recommendation,
central to Butler's view of the 'moral universe' which requires
that a man, in order to deserve the description of being a moral
agent, must be such that he feels benevolently towards his
fellows, and acts benevolently towards them. A man who consistently responds benevolently develops a dispositional tendency and we recognise in him the benevolent man.

Butler's famous disagreement with Hobbes concerning the
status of benevolence can be seen either as a conceptual disagreement or a disagreement of moral viewpoint. Butler, in his
long note to the first sermon, 'Upon Human Nature',[70] takes
up Hobbes's attempt to deny the existence of benevolence by
interpreting the motive for alleged benevolent actions in terms
of the love of the exercise of power over others. Butler's first

move here is to counter Hobbes by making a conceptual point: what Hobbes calls 'benevolence' is an action motivated by the love of the exercise of power over another, but this is not at all Butler's definition of benevolence. 'Would not everybody think here was a mistake of one word for another? that the philosopher was contemplating and accounting for some other human actions, some other behaviour of man to man?'[71]

But if Hobbes refuses to accept Butler's point that they are disagreeing about the application of words, and if Hobbes insists that the *same* thing or action which Butler describes as 'benevolent', he describes as 'motivated by a love of power', the disagreement is no longer logical, but moral. Butler wants to suggest it is a factual disagreement by claiming that it is a fact that we act more benevolently towards our friends than towards strangers, and on Hobbes's analysis, this amounts to a greater love in us of exercising power over our friends than over strangers. And this, argues Butler, is absurd. Hobbes's proposed substitution of 'love of power over another' for 'benevolence' therefore fails abysmally.

But Hobbes's analysis is only absurd if we accept Butler's interpretation of the fact that we act more benevolently towards friends than towards strangers. Butler is mistaken in implying that Hobbes's analysis leads him to deny that it is a fact that we act more benevolently towards friends than towards strangers. *This* fact is not in dispute: what is in dispute is its interpretation. Butler says; we act more benevolently towards our friends because we feel more benevolently towards them. Hobbes retorts: we act more benevolently towards our friends because we delight more in the exercise of power over them. And this disagreement cannot be settled by an appeal to the 'facts': it is a disagreement involving moral viewpoints, in particular one concerning rival assessments of human nature.

We must now discuss the question much debated by commentators on Butler's moral philosophy, namely whether he identifies benevolence with virtue. It is reasonably clear that in Butler's *Dissertation on the Nature of Virtue* published with the *Analogy* in 1736, he quite definitely does not identify benevolence with virtue. He writes: 'Without inquiring how far, and in what sense, virtue is resolvable into benevolence, and vice into the want of it; it may be proper to observe, that benevolence, and the want of it, singly considered, are in no sort the whole of virtue and vice.'[72] Arguing against the view that benevolence is the whole of virtue, he points out that if benevolence aims at bringing about 'an overbalance of happiness over misery' this would make it right that 'one man, by fraud or violence, take from another the fruit of his labour, with intent to give it to a third, who he thought would have as much pleasure out of it as would balance the pleasure which the first possessor would have had in the enjoyment, and his vexation in the loss of it; suppose also that no bad consequences would follow.'[73] Such an action would however be unquestionably condemned by our moral faculty. 'We are constituted so as to condemn falsehood, unprovoked violence, injustice, and to approve of benevolence to some preferably to others, abstracted from all consideration, which conduct is likeliest to produce an overbalance of happiness or misery.'[74] Even if, argues Butler, God's purpose for the creation is the production of happiness, this is not the 'end' of human nature. 'This is our constitution: falsehood, violence, injustice must be vice in us, and benevolence to some, preferably to others, virtue; abstracted from all consideration of the overbalance of evil or good, which they may appear likely to produce.'[75]

Butler's position in the *Sermons* is more problematic. T. H. McPherson has maintained[76] that in the *Sermons* Butler is an 'ethical eudaemonist', that is, one who believes that the happiness-producing character of actions is what makes them right. This thesis was expressed by Sidgwick but McPherson has argued the case by examining the text in greater detail. In effect it leads to identifying virtue with happiness. Opposed to it is the more traditional interpretation, expressed in recent times by C. D. Broad,[77] and A. E. Taylor,[78] that Butler's position in the *Sermons* does not substantially differ from that adopted in the *Dissertation*; this is that conscience discerns what is right and wrong, and the fact that conscience decrees an action right or wrong constitutes the ground of its rightness or wrongness, which is not based on its happiness-producing characteristics. On this view, virtue is not to be identified with benevolence. A third possible interpretation has been advocated by A. R. White. He supports the traditional interpretation which holds that for Butler conscience declares which actions are right or wrong, without regard to their consequences assessed in terms of the production of happiness. However, White takes into account Butler's repeated references in the *Sermons* to happiness as man's supreme end in order to suggest that Butler believed man requires a motive for doing what is right, and this motive is his desire to obtain happiness.

Is it possible to come down on one side or another in this debate? Examination of the *Sermons* produces indisputable evidence to support both points of view. In his analysis of conscience, Butler states categorically, in the words which frequent quotation has made so familiar, that 'there is a superior principle of reflection or conscience in every man which distinguishes between the internal principles of his heart, as well as his external actions . . . pronounces determinately some actions to be in themselves just, right, good. . . .'[79] The quotations given above from the *Dissertation* in which Butler holds that we approve some actions and disapprove others 'abstracted from all consideration which conduct is likeliest to produce an overbalance of happiness or misery' is a further statement and elaboration of a standpoint expressed unequivocally in the discussion on conscience, namely that we possess a faculty which pronounces some actions to be, *in themselves*,[80] just, right and good. Moreover, since conscience is supreme over all the subordinate affections and passions, it is supreme over benevolence, so that the end of benevolence, the happiness of others, must be made subordinate and subservient to conscience.

On the other hand, in his discussion of benevolence, Butler states equally categorically that 'benevolence in the strict sense seems to include in it all that is good and worthy': he implies it is the 'sum of virtue'; it is the 'temper of virtue' and the 'common virtues and vices may be traced to benevolence'.

It seems then, that in the *Sermons* at least, Butler's views on the relation between benevolence and virtue are inconsistent and incompatible. He seems to be holding on one hand that the criteria of what is virtuous, are the pronouncements of conscience, and on the other that the criterion of virtue is benevolence, and benevolence aims at actions whose consequences bring about the happiness of others. In Butler's favour it can be argued that by the time he came to write the *Dissertation* and the *Analogy of Religion*, he had resolved the conflict, for in those works it is beyond dispute that the former is his view – we identify virtue as what conscience declares to be right.

It is possible to argue however that Butler's views about the relation between virtue and benevolence are not inconsistent. Virtue, he holds, lies in acting in accordance with one's nature. Happiness or satisfaction, he maintains, 'consists only in the enjoyment of those objects which are by nature suited to our several particular appetites, passions and affections'.[81] So if we act according to our nature we act virtuously, and we also achieve happiness. The question arises, whose happiness is achieved, our own or that of others? As Butler holds that the deepest satisfaction to the self comes from doing those actions which achieve the happiness of others, by acting benevolently we bring about not only the happiness of others but our own greatest happiness, and as this is also acting in accordance with our nature, we are acting virtuously. The apparent inconsistency, it could be argued, is removed from Butler's thought.

Ingenious as this argument is, it does not succeed, for it does little to meet the difficulty that arises from Butler's clear statement that conscience pronounces some actions to be in themselves right or just, without regard to their consequences in maximising happiness. This view remains a stumbling block for anyone who seeks to reconcile Butler's views on virtue and benevolence.

The inconsistency in his views on the relation between virtue and happiness is not the only criticism that we can offer on Butler's analysis of benevolence. For example, in saying that benevolence seeks the good of another, which is to be interpreted in terms of maximising his happiness, it is not clear whether Butler is making a conceptual point or offering a value judgement. If benevolence is to be defined as acting for the happiness of another, he is best understood to be making a conceptual point, from which it would follow that if we act for the sake of something other than the happiness of another, we are not acting benevolently. On the other hand, if we define benevolence as acting for the good of others, Butler could then be interpreted as recommending the value judgement that by the good of another we are to understand his happiness.

Again when Butler reconciles his ideas of self-love and benevolence by insisting that what the self finds genuinely satisfying, and so fulfils the aims of self-love, is acting so as to secure the happiness of another, it is difficult to decide whether he is recommending a particular definition of 'self-love' or whether he is suggesting that self-love be defined as seeking the real interest of the self and that, for Butler, it is a value judgement that this real interest lies in acting for the sake of the happiness of others.

In holding that benevolence has to do with maximising happiness, Butler does not consider how the concept of happiness is to be understood. In this he reflects a weakness which is evident also in Mill's utilitarianism, although he does not identify pleasure and happiness in the crude way that Mill does. But like Mill, Butler does not consider whether there can be more than one kind of happiness, or whether one can identify happiness with what one wants. But even assuming that we can all agree on the same analysis of happiness, whatever that is, Butler does not consider how one decides between different courses of action which produce the same amount of happiness; for example, if an action A makes six men supremely happy whereas action B makes twelve men moderately happy, how should we choose between them, assuming the total sum of happiness produced by A and B is the same?

3   Hume's Discussion of Benevolence in the *Treatise*

The two most important sources for Hume's discussion of benevolence are his *Treatise of Human Nature*, and his *Enquiry Concerning the Principles of Morals* which was published in 1751. The first two books of the *Treatise* were published in 1739 and the third book in 1740. Hume regarded the *Enquiry Concerning the Principles of Morals*, of all his writings, 'historical, philosophical, or literary, incomparably the best'. Its substance is drawn from the third book of the *Treatise* but it is presented, with some changes, in a more pleasing and attractive style.[1] How far the difference between the two works is merely a matter of style and slight change of content is a question that need not detain us in the present task of following Hume's views on benevolence as set out in the *Treatise*.

The main topics of Hume's discussion in the *Treatise* which we need to note are (*a*) the relation of benevolence to the indirect passions, especially love, (*b*) sympathy and benevolence and (*c*) benevolence and justice.

1. *Benevolence and the Indirect Passions*

The second book of the *Treatise* is entitled 'Of the Passions' and in it Hume sets out to analyse the important emotions – pride, joy, fear, humility, love, hatred, generosity – which human beings commonly feel. Book II is meant as an essential prologomenon to Book III, entitled 'Of Morals', which discusses several important topics in moral philosophy, and in particular centres on Hume's analysis of moral judgement in terms of moral sentiments. Hume's essay in psychology in Book II admirably fulfils his intention, expressed in the subtitle to the *Treatise*, namely that it is 'an attempt to introduce the experimental method of reasoning into moral subjects'. At many points in his discussion of the emotions Hume frequently puts forward a claim for consideration as a hypothesis which he believes can be verified by our own reflection on our experience of these emotions. As Butler's discussion of benevolence is a refinement on that of Hutcheson's, not least in his more detailed analysis of compassion, so Hume's is a more comprehensive, wide-ranging and philosophically more fruitful discussion (even though some commentators have claimed that Book II is of no philosophical value) than that of either Hutcheson or Butler from both of whom, no doubt, he did not hesitate to borrow such ideas as seemed useful to him. Like Hutcheson and Butler, his approach is empiricist, and the presuppositions of his psychological analysis are Cartesian in the sense that he believes emotions and feelings are private experiences, in which the relation between a feeling and its object is contingent.

In his discussion of the 'influencing motives of the will'[2] Hume writes:

> Now 'tis certain, there are certain calm desires and tendencies, which, tho' they be real passions, produce little emotion in the mind, and are more known by their effects than by the immediate feeling or sensation. These desires are of two kinds: either certain instincts originally implanted in our natures, such as benevolence and resentment, the love of life, and kindness to children; or the general appetite to good, and aversion to evil, consider'd merely as such.[3]

In this quotation, in which we have Hume's first mention, in Book II, of benevolence, the latter is classified as a 'calm passion'. To understand this classification of benevolence as a calm passion, we require to know something of Hume's division of the passions.

Hume starts with the basic assumption set out in Book I, that all mental states, that is all states or modes of mind, are perceptions, and perceptions are either impressions or ideas. Ideas are copies of impressions, differing from them only in vivacity. Impressions are divided into original, and secondary or reflective impressions. Original impressions are either sensations (that is, states of mind not derived from other impressions or ideas, but caused by the impact of external objects on our senses) or bodily pains or pleasures, whose causes are internal physiological or psychological states. Secondary or reflective impressions arise from an original impression or its idea. The passions or emotions are, in general, classed as secondary impressions. Two further sub-divisions are introduced by Hume: first the distinction between the calm and the violent passions – the sense of beauty and deformity in action is instanced as an example of a calm passion, whereas love, hatred, grief, joy, pride and humility are examples of violent passions; the second is the distinction between the direct and the indirect passions, the differentiating criterion being that a direct passion 'arises immediately from pleasure or pain', and the indirect passion 'proceeds from the same principle, but by the conjunction of other qualities'. Desire, aversion, grief, joy, hope, fear, despair and security are examples of direct passions, a classification which overlaps with the previous one of 'violent passions', whereas pride, humility, ambition, love, hatred, envy, pity, malice, vanity and generosity are examples of the indirect passions, and this class again overlaps with that of the violent passions. Most of Book II is concerned with an analysis of the indirect passions.

In this classification, which Hume presents in the introductory section to Book II, there is no reference to benevolence. Moreover it clearly implies that the distinction between the calm and the violent, the direct and indirect applies only to the secondary impressions and not to the original impressions, for the passions or emotions arise directly or indirectly from precedent pleasures and pains. The reference in the quotation given above to benevolence both as one of the 'original instincts implanted in our nature' and as a calm desire suggests that Hume has not consistently followed his classification of the passions set out in his introduction to Book II.

In his discussion of the indirect passions, to which, as we have noted, most of Book II is devoted, Hume is concerned to distinguish between the cause of, the sensation or feeling of, and the object of, an indirect passion. What then for Hume are the cause, the sensation or feeling associated with, and the object of benevolence?

Unlike an indirect passion, benevolence does not arise from an original impression or idea, for it is itself an 'original instinct' in human nature. If benevolence is an original impression, then it is not strictly a passion, for passions are reflective impressions whose existence presupposes precedent original impressions.

However, Hume does refer to benevolence as a passion. We can interpret Hume in one of two ways. We can either stress Hume's reference to benevolence as an original instinct in human nature and insist that, strictly, Hume cannot include it under the passions: or else we can say it is one of the passions, and that therefore it is an exception to Hume's claim that all passions presuppose the existence of precedent original impressions or their ideas. Whichever interpretation is adopted Hume wishes to hold that benevolence has no cause by way of a precedent impression, and in this it differs from the passions; although its existence as a mode of mind in a particular individual has a physical or physiological cause (or causes), but Hume specifically excludes from his account any discussion of what these causes might be. Benevolence, apart from the sensations of pleasure and pain, is not alone in being an original instinct in this sense, for, in the quotation already given, resentment, love of life, and affection to children are classed with benevolence as 'original instincts'.

By maintaining that benevolence is an original instinct implanted in our nature, Hume wishes to claim that this 'passion', this 'feeling' element in human nature which is the motive (i.e. the cause) of a certain type of action (i.e. benevolent action), is brought into existence or caused neither by the prior existence in the mind of some other 'feeling' element such as another passion, nor by a sensation of pleasure or pain, nor by an impression (or its idea) brought into existence by some state of affairs external to the individual. Thus benevolence for Hume is not, for instance, akin to compassion for Butler, for whom the affection of compassion is brought into existence by the sight of others in distress. True to his empiricist psychology, Hume holds that action can only be motivated by the 'impulse of passion', which reason can never produce, only at best direct,[4] and so benevolent actions are motivated by this 'impulse' which Hume calls benevolence. That it exists, and does motivate human actions, is a brute but contingent fact about human nature. We are, on Hume's analysis, unable to offer any explanation or account of its existence beyond drawing attention to it. It follows from Hume's analysis that if the existence of the 'impulse' or 'passion' of benevolence is a contingent fact about human nature as it is now constituted, it would be impossible to conceive human beings, possessing the nature they now possess, lacking this impulse or passion of benevolence, though of course it would be possible to conceive of a human nature very different from ours which lacked benevolence. A possible objector to Hume's analysis could therefore plausibly contend that, even if we grant the contingent fact that benevolence is part of human nature as now constituted, it would be theoretically possible, by means of education, propaganda, and by creating conditioning factors in the environment, to produce human beings who possessed the human nature we now possess but who never acted benevolently nor felt this impulse or passion.

As for the feeling or sensation which accompanies the impulse or passion of benevolence, Hume confesses in the quotation already given that 'little emotion in the mind' is associated with this passion. We only know of its existence from its effects. This reference to 'little emotion' accompanying the impulse immediately invites the retort, how little is little? Apart from the problem of specifying the criteria for distinguishing between a little and a great deal of emotion, Hume's claim that the existence of benevolence as a motive for action is known from its effects leaves the question open concerning the specific nature of the motive. Hume's general empiricist analysis of the psychology of human nature predetermines the answer to the question, what kind of thing is this thing in the mind which motivates action we describe or recognise as benevolent? For Hume, it must be 'an impulse or passion' which is, contingently, accompanied by very little emotion or feeling. This answer has all the appearances of an empirical statement of fact, and it is not to be overlooked that Hume conceived his task in general to be applying the experimental method of science, based on hypothesis and observation, to the field of the psychology of mind, but his answer is one influenced more by his empiricist presuppositions than based upon an attempt to describe objectively what is the case. Indeed a conceptual problem lies at the root of Hume's difficulties. If the impulse or passion of benevolence is, contingently, associated with so little emotion that we cannot recognise it from its accompanying emotion or sensation, then how is it to be recognised? At this point in his discussion Hume offers no criteria of identification, but infers the existence of the benevolent impulse in us from its effects, i.e. from benevolent actions. But the claim, essential to Hume's analysis of the status of benevolence, that actions are motivated by impulses or passions, is not made on the basis of empirical investigation or observation; it lies already implicit in the conceptual framework of his empiricist psychology.

Two of the three questions Hume thinks can be asked about a passion – namely, what is its cause, and what is the nature of the sensation or feeling associated with it – have been discussed. There remains the third of his questions – what is the object of benevolence?

In considering this latter question, we must first ask, what does Hume mean by an 'object' in this context? If we turn to his account of the indirect passions of pride and humility, we learn that the 'object' of both is the self. Thus pride and humility are contrasted with love and hatred where the object is said to be some other person (or persons) and not the self. The distinction in Hume's mind seems to be that if X says he loves his father, two things, at least, can be noted of this state of affairs:

(*a*) the loving is predicated of X
(*b*) X's loving is directed towards his father.

If now X says he is proud of his father, then we can say:

(*a*) the being proud is predicated of X
(*b*) the pride of X is directed towards himself (not towards his father).

Thus pride is different from love in being directed towards the person who possesses the passion.[5]

Hume's notion of the 'object' of a passion as that to which it is directed is not without its difficulties. If both love and hatred are directed towards other persons, then in one sense they both possess the same 'object' but since 'love' and 'hatred' are different passions, they must possess, not the same, but different 'objects', and this we can allow if we specify the object of each more closely than Hume does, as love seeks the happiness, or what is believed conducive to the happiness, of others, whereas hatred seeks what is harmful to others. Again Hume's designation of the object, in such an expression as 'the object of pride', as 'that towards which the emotion is directed' seems arbitrary, for in one quite acceptable use of the term 'object', it is possible to refer to the father as the proper object of pride in the expression 'he is proud of his father'.

However, disregarding the difficulties of Hume's notion of the 'object' of a passion, we note that for him the object of benevolence is some person (or persons) other than the possessor of the passion. In this respect, benevolence resembles love and is unlike pride, for benevolence is directed towards other persons. If we ask which persons, Hume is quite adamant in replying that the class of persons towards whom benevolence can be directed is relatively restricted: it includes a person's relatives, his friends, and then a somewhat wider class of persons with whom one has some recognisable and significant relation, as for example a person who is a complete stranger but happens to be one's only fellow national in a foreign country. As the class of people towards whom benevolence can be directed widens, so the impulse or passion becomes progressively weaker, so that when the circle is enlarged to include the whole of mankind, the passion to act benevolently weakens almost to vanishing point.

Hume's conception of the 'object' of benevolence raises two considerations that merit attention. Firstly, in asserting that benevolence has an object, Hume is undeniably thinking of that impulse or passion which exists and motivates a particular benevolent action, and his notion of the object of benevolence relates to that to which the action is directed. As in ordinary language we undoubtedly do use the adjectival and adverbial forms of the noun, 'benevolence', to describe certain actions, as for example 'he acted benevolently' or 'his was a benevolent act', Hume's account of the 'object' of benevolence can be understood as an attempt to offer, in part, an analysis of our use of the terms 'benevolently' and 'benevolent' when qualified of actions; for their correct use, on Hume's account, presupposes the existence in the agent of the impulse or passion of benevolence. But even if Hume is correct in asserting this, ordinary language also allows us to predicate the adjective 'benevolent' of a person's character, or trait of character, as when we imply someone possesses a disposition to act benevolently. This latter use does not however presuppose the existence of an impulse or passion of benevolence present in a particular person at any and every moment; its use implies that a person frequently or regularly acts benevolently as circumstances require. Hume's analysis does not allow for ordinary language's sanction of this latter use of 'benevolent', though of course it does imply that when the benevolent man acts benevolently, then his action is motivated by an impulse or passion of benevolence existing as a state of mind.

The second point is this. When Hume claims that the 'object' of benevolence is some person or persons other than the self, is he making an empirical claim or establishing a conceptual truth? It seems clear that Hume believed he was stating an empirical fact about the nature of something that exists as a state of mind and motivates an act of benevolence. Leaving aside the difficulty of understanding how this state of mind can have an 'object', let us assume that the object of benevolence is, contingently, some person or persons other than the self, as Hume maintains. If this is contingently the case, it must be possible to conceive or imagine a quite different human nature, existing in some other world than ours, in which the 'object' of benevolence is, contingently, one's own self. But is it in fact possible to conceive of an impulse, directed towards the good of the self which could be named 'benevolence'? Surely such an impulse would be termed self-love, and could not (logically) be termed 'benevolence' unless that word is to lose the meaning it now possesses in ordinary language We must conclude that, despite the use of such expressions as 'I'll be generous to myself by . . .', which imply benevolence towards oneself, but which are parasitic on the notion of acting benevolently towards others, it is a conceptual truth, not a contingent fact, that the 'object' of benevolence is some person or persons not the self. Hume believed otherwise, and thought he was establishing an empirical fact, and his error provides yet another example of how he was misled by his empiricist frame of thinking.

2. *Benevolence and Love*

Despite its many weaknesses, Hume's analysis of the passions is more comprehensive and philosophically interesting than anything produced by his eighteenth-century contemporaries, and in the matter of benevolence it raises questions concerning the relation between love and benevolence, sympathy and benevolence, and justice and benevolence. The first of these topics will be briefly discussed in this section.

According to Hume, love is one of the indirect passions; that is, an impression arising from a precedent impression of pleasure, together with the existence of certain qualities or characteristics in that which arouses the impression or passion. His classification of love with the indirect passions presupposes the general validity of his doctrine of the double relation of impressions and ideas, which is the psychological mechanism Hume invokes to account, in conformity with the relation of cause and effect, for the way passions arise in the human breast. I do not propose to examine in detail Hume's doctrine of the double relation of impressions and ideas, since it is derived from Hume's empiricist epistemology developed in terms of impressions of sense and of ideas which are less vivid copies of impressions. Impressions of sense are, for Hume, identifiable with states of mind brought into existence by the effect upon the senses of external or internal (physiological or psychological) objects, and ideas – ideas being another set or class of states of mind, which are in some sense less vivid copies of impressions. Hume's general epistemological framework, of which the doctrine of the double relation of impressions and ideas forms a part, is vulnerable precisely because it assumes the possibility of analysing items of conceptual awareness in consciousness into items or elements derived exclusively from sense experience. Those who reject this possibility must also reject the basis of Hume's epistemology.

In addition to his doctrine of the double relation of impressions and ideas, there is another general epistemological thesis which underlies Hume's discussion of the passions, and of love in particular. This is the thesis, which need not be examined in detail here, that all the passions are simple impressions. By 'simple' impression Hume seems to mean an impression that cannot be analysed into parts. However, he does not intend to imply by this that the only thing we can do with a simple impression is to point to it and name it. He believes it is possible to observe similarities between simple impressions, and indeed this similarity of impressions is essential for the principle of association which he uses to account for the causal explanation we can offer of the conditions which give rise to any particular passion or impression, or emotion. That the passions are simple impressions presupposes the more general claim that some impressions are simple. This in turn raises the question of what is meant by holding that an impression is simple, and in particular it raises the question whether anything that is simple can be similar to something else. If X is similar to Y, it is possible to argue that in that case X cannot be simple but must be complex, for X must consist of what is similar to Y, and what is different from Y, otherwise it would be identical with Y. If the notion of what is similar conceptually excludes the notion of being simple, there is a logical flaw at the root of Hume's analysis of the passions as simple impressions. Thus Professor J. A. Passmore concludes that from the claim that simples resemble each other in being simple, Hume should have realised that there are no simples.[6]

Even if Hume's general epistemological framework, in which he locates his discussion of love and benevolence, is untenable, it may still remain true that in distinguishing between them, he succeeds in drawing attention to interesting conceptual points of similarity and difference between them. To turn to his analysis of love, Hume considers the matter under three main headings, namely, the nature of the emotion, its object, and its cause. Let us examine each in turn.

With regard to the particular nature of the sensation of the emotion of love, Hume claims that its nature is sufficiently known from 'our common feeling or experience'. The juxtaposition of the two words 'feeling' and 'experience' in this expression is itself significant, for it implies that experience is accompanied by feeling, an implication which comes naturally to Hume's empiricist outlook, though one should not adopt his outlook uncritically. This feeling of love is agreeable and is described by Hume as similar to 'that tender emotion which is excited by a friend or mistress'.[7] He assumes there exists a specific sensation associated with the emotion of love, an inward sensation separately identifiable from other sensations, and distinguishable from its effects. In other words, Hume assumes that love is externally related to its object. The fact that he was unable to describe or specify more closely the kind of sensation that love is suggests that love is not, as Hume mistakenly believes, externally related, but is internally related to its object. Thus in his example of the love of a mistress, we cannot describe or specify the nature of this love independently of, or without reference to, its object.

Hume declares that the 'object' of love, that to which the emotion is directed, is some other thinking person (or persons) of whose 'thoughts, actions and sensations we are not conscious'.[8] On Hume's general epistemological analysis, we are not, and cannot be, directly conscious of the states of mind of another person, for we are only directly conscious of our own states of mind. He lays this down as axiomatic, and does not really consider the possibility that we may be directly conscious of another's state of mind. Nor does he discuss whether the fact that one is only directly conscious of one's own state of mind is a contingent fact or a conceptual truth. On Hume's analysis our knowledge of the states of mind of other persons is inferred. In holding that the object of love can only be another thinking person, Hume wishes to distinguish between a person and an inanimate object, for he contends that a particular quality in an inanimate object does not excite love in the way that the same quality in an individual does. Thus beauty in a house or possession does not arouse love, but beauty in a person does or can excite it.[9] He does not consider whether the same quality in an animal can excite love.

It is clear that in thinking of the object of love Hume thinks it possible to separate the emotion or sensation from its object and describe the latter independently of the former. The object is always, he holds, some other thinking person or persons. This leads him to exclude self-love, of which 'we cannot properly talk', on the grounds that the sensation characteristic of self-love is not the same kind of sensation as that 'tender emotion excited by a friend or mistress'. This presupposes that one can separately identify the two different emotions of love and self-love, and that the 'tender emotion excited by a friend or mistress' is accepted as typical of the emotion manifested by love. Both assumptions are questionable, but they are forced on Hume by his conviction that the description of an emotion is externally related to the description of its object, and that one can indeed furnish a description of the one independently of the other. The belief that the characteristic nature of the emotion of love is typified by what is excited by a friend or mistress leads him to exclude the possibility of loving an in-animate object, and this exclusion is arbitrary.

What account does Hume give of the 'cause' of love, that is, of what excites the emotion in us? First, the cause must be some quality or qualities in another person (or persons) and not in ourselves or in inanimate objects. These qualities can be very numerous and diverse in nature, 'which do not have many things in common'. Wisely Hume does not attempt an exhaustive classification of the causes of love. In general he is content to distinguish between these qualities or characteristics in a person which we judge agreeable or useful. Both arouse our love, except that Hume qualifies this with regard to actions that are agreeable or useful to us by saying that in order to arouse love these actions must be intentional. If someone does good to us, we take his good actions to signify his kind intentions towards us, and this arouses our love: if on the other hand we discover that in doing good to us, he acted accidentally or inadvertently, his actions, even though agreeable or useful to us, are no longer such as to arouse our love towards him.

In addition to the agreeable or useful qualities or characteristics of a person, or the useful or agreeable actions, both of which arouse our love, Hume thinks that the emotion of love is remarkable in that 'it may be excited by only one relation of a different kind, viz. betwixt ourselves and the object'.[10] In other words, the operation of the double relation of impression and ideas which Hume posits as the mechanism involved when emotions are aroused is not essential in the case of love, so that in this regard love is different from the other indirect passions. Hume believes that if we are related to another person (or persons) by ties of kinship or country, then love towards that person is aroused in proportion to the strength of that relation, 'without enquiring into his other qualities', that is, irrespective of whether his qualities or actions are useful or agreeable. Thus: 'We love our country-men, our neighbours, those of the same trade, profession, and even name with ourselves. Everyone of these relations is esteemed some tie, and gives a title to a share of our affection.'[11] Blood relation produces the strongest tie but acquaintance without any kind of blood relation gives rise to some love.

In drawing attention to the exceptional character of love, namely that a relation between a person and another and not some lovable qualities in one of them can arouse love, Hume overlooks the fact that acquaintance is frequently insufficient to arouse or sustain love, in the absence of lovable qualities in the loved one. Ties of acquaintance may give rise to interest or fellow-feeling but hardly to love. Similarly the blood tie is of itself frequently insufficient either to arouse or to sustain love. Despite the strong blood bond, a man may come to hate his father or mother, brother or sister, or he may at least come to cease to love them. A blood tie is in itself no guarantee of love. Love founded on acquaintance is likely to wither unless, on deeper acquaintance, one comes to learn of the lovable qualities of the loved one. In considering the love that is founded on blood ties, Hume has not discussed the possibility that love is not destroyed when the person loved changes his character and acquires less desirable and unlovable qualities. A mother does not cease to love her child who undoubtedly once possessed attractive qualities when later in life he becomes vicious and unattractive. Hume seems to discuss the emotion of love as if there was only one kind of love, namely the tender emotion that arises between lovers and friends, whereas in reality expressions of love are almost infinite in variety.

Hume emphasises that love is closely related to pride in the sense that the same qualities which in one person arouse our love towards him give rise to pride when they are present in us. According to Hume, pride differs from love in always having the self, and not other persons, as its object. The validity of his claim concerning the close relation of love and pride turns very much on the criteria of what constitutes 'agreeable and useful qualities'. These criteria Hume does not state, although he believes agreeable and useful qualities in others arouse our love of them. If 'agreeable' and 'useful' were defined in relation to the good of society, it would be possible to imagine a person being proud of some characteristic or action of his which would not be regarded as useful and agreeable to society, though he might think them useful to himself. A misguided man can be proud of his criminal achievements although his criminal tendencies or traits of character cannot be regarded as being useful or agreeable to society. Hume's claim that the qualities which arouse pride in the human breast are the very same qualities which in another arouse our love cannot therefore be sustained.

In his analysis of the causes of the emotion of love Hume seems to accept the assumption, somewhat mechanistic in its nature and central to his empiricist psychology, that the same stimulus elicits a similar response. Thus the quality or characteristic of beauty in one person uniformly and consistently arouses love of it in another person. Now whereas it may be generally true of the particular quality of beauty that its presence in another arouses love of it in us, it is not true that it invariably does so in all persons. Some are unmoved by beauty, and some envy its presence in others. This is also true of other qualities or traits of character. None of them invariably arouse a similar response in different people. In short Hume's mechanistic analysis of love has led him to overlook the fact that what a person loves is internally related to what he admires or thinks highly of, and individuals differ enormously in what they admire. What one admires is repulsive to another, so that one man's meat is another's poison. Differences in taste, differences in likes and dislikes, and above all differences in moral attitudes or beliefs, must be taken into account in any attempt to explain how persons differ in what they admire and love. A person's likes or dislikes are closely connected with his beliefs or convictions about what is, in Hume's phrase, 'agreeable and useful', and beliefs about what is agreeable and useful establish the criteria of excellence with regard to these qualities. Thus differences in beliefs between one person and another will be crucially relevant to any account of why individuals differ in what they admire or love. Sometimes differences of belief involve differences of moral belief, so that one man may admire what to another is morally unworthy. A pacifist cannot believe that war in any circumstances is justified, although war against Hitler who was responsible for crimes against the Jews may be excusable. A non-pacifist may think that Hitler's crimes against humanity justified going to war against him, so that in Cromwell's phrase, he rejoices in knowing why he goes to war, and loves what he knows. Here we have fundamental differences in moral belief so that the pacifist abhors what, in some sense, the non-pacifist comes to love. Hume's determination to analyse the emotions entirely in the light of his empiricist conviction that the mind associates the constant experience of one stimulus with an equally constant experience of the corresponding response of feeling or emotion, blinds him to the role that beliefs must play in any analysis of the emotions, and this is nowhere more evident than in his discussion of the causes of emotions, and in particular, those of the emotion of love.

In Section VI,[12] Hume considers the connection between love and benevolence. Thus he writes: 'The passions of love and hatred are always followed by, or rather conjoin'd with benevolence and anger. 'Tis this conjunction, which chiefly distinguishes these affections from pride and humility.'[13]

A somewhat dubious and artificial comparison of ideas to extension and solidity in matter, whereby Hume claims that ideas 'are endow'd with a kind of impenetrability',[14] and a further distinction in this regard between ideas on the one hand, which are not, and impression or passions which are, 'susceptible of an entire union', precedes the claim that love is a passion conjoined with benevolence.

Love, according to Hume, differs from pride in that the latter is a 'pure emotion'. His criteria of a pure emotion are that it is 'unattended with any desire, and not immediately exciting us to action'. Love and hatred on the other hand 'are not compleated within themselves, nor rest in that emotion, which they produce, but carry the mind to something else'. Love is always followed by 'the desire of the happiness of the person belov'd and an aversion to his misery'. Hume argues that the desire for the happiness of the one loved is not essential to the emotion of love, but follows when the idea of the happiness of the person loved is presented by the imagination to the mind. Although the desire for the happiness of the person loved always follows upon the emotion of love, Hume considers that this is a contingent fact. He believes therefore that the emotion of love, and the desire for the happiness of the person loved, are two separate passions which he calls love and benevolence. The conjoining of love and benevolence in human nature is due, contingently, to the original constitution of the mind. Hume thus sees no difficulty in conceiving a state of affairs where the emotion of love is followed, not by the desire for the happiness of the beloved, but by a desire for his misery. As he puts it, 'If nature had so pleas'd, love might have had the same effect as hatred, and hatred as love.'[15]

Hume's argument in this short section merits brief comment. First, we can concede to him that there is no difficulty in conceiving nature as very different from what in fact it is. There is also no difficulty in conceiving that the English language might be very different from what it now is, so that the word 'love' meant what 'hatred' now means. There is a sense in which it is arbitrary that we use the word 'love' for love. But it is difficult to understand how love (whatever symbol in whatever language is used to refer to it) could have the effects of hatred. And this is a conceptual difficulty. If there existed in human nature an emotion followed by the effects of hatred, we would be at a loss to know by which word we would refer to it, unless it is the word 'hatred'. It is not therefore as Hume thinks, a question of whether human nature could be different from what it now is. Human nature could be different, and might be one that lacked the emotion of love. But what is understood by love would be unchanged; the difference would be that in another world there might not be instances of the concept of love. Hume's error lies in thinking that an emotion can be separately and independently identified from its effects, so that the connection between the emotion and its effects is contingent. This can only be so if the relation between the description of the emotion and the description of its effects is, as Hume mistakenly implies, external, and not internal.

Although Hume's psychological analysis leads him to distinguish, somewhat unsatisfactorily, between pure passions which are not conjoined with other passions, and the passions which, like love and benevolence, are conjoined, he does in spite of this mistaken analysis point to a conceptual truth about love, provided we restate what Hume says. Love is an emotion that can be felt in varying degrees. We can love one person intensely, while loving another less so. The concept of love does seem to imply that, in the standard case of a person loving another, he wants to seek the good of the beloved, that is, it implies wanting very much to act benevolently towards the beloved. This is obviously not true of all cases of loving, for where the affection is weak, as when love grows cold, there may not exist a very strong desire to act benevolently towards the beloved. By saying however that the passions of love and benevolence are always conjoined, Hume seems to imply that it is true of all instances of loving that they are accompanied by strong desires to act benevolently towards the beloved. But since this is not always so, Hume's model of the two passions always being conjoined together is misleading.

If the standard instance of loving another implies acting benevolently towards the beloved, we can ask whether the relation between love and benevolence is symmetrical, in the sense that an instance of benevolence is also an instance of love, as an instance of love is also an instance of benevolence. If Jones acts benevolently towards Mary, does this imply that Jones loves Mary? Hume does not specifically discuss this question. He does however suggest that the kind of emotion associated with each of these passions is not the same. According to Hume, love possesses its own characteristic tender emotion, though he hardly describes it in such a way that we could always and unmistakably recognise it. Benevolence on the other hand is, according to Hume, accompanied by such a weak degree of emotion that we can only recognise the passion from its effects; that is, the existence of the passion is inferred from the character of the actions expressive of the passion. Here again Hume's account is based on a misconceived psychology which forces him to argue for the existence of an emotion which can hardly be felt. Despite his mistaken psychology, Hume may be pointing to something which is true. What he may be driving at is the claim that if Jones acts benevolently towards Mary, this entails that he feels benevolently disposed towards her. However, the expression 'feels benevolently disposed towards someone' is not particularly illuminating until it is recognised as a description which can be used to cover a number of possibilities ranging at one extreme from a desire to act generously towards someone to whom one has no special obligation to act generously, through active concern for another's welfare, as when the distress of someone may arouse compassionate concern, to the strongly felt emotion of tenderness which the lover feels for the beloved, towards whom he acts benevolently. Thus the standard description of a person acting benevolently towards someone does not entail that the agent loves the person who is the object of the benevolence, whereas the standard description of a person loving another does seem to imply that the lover desires to act for the happiness or good of the beloved.

3. *Benevolence and Sympathy*

Sympathy, maintains Hume, is 'nothing but a lively idea converted into an impression'.[16] As it stands this is not very informative, beyond presupposing his cardinal distinction between ideas and impressions and, on the face of it, controverting his general thesis that ideas are derived from impressions. To get at Hume's meaning, we need to get the quotation in the context of his thought. Hume is discussing 'the transition of the passions'. That is, in relation to his general analysis of the passions or emotions, he is seeking to account for the fact that one person can be affected by another's emotion, and sympathy is in the first instance, Hume's term for his account of the psychological process whereby one person's emotion is communicated to another, so that he also feels it. Sympathy involves the way in which my idea or conception (Hume's terminology) of another's emotion is transformed into my impression, that is, into a felt experience of the same emotion as the other is feeling, of which I have an idea. Thus Hume seeks to explain how, for example, if John feels sorrow, Mary comes to feel sorrow at his sorrow, and this process he calls sympathy (although of course it is not confined just to feeling sorrow, for emotions like fear, pride, love and so on can also be communicated).

In order to understand the psychological mechanism by which sympathy functions, we must note the following features which, on Hume's account, an emotion possesses. First, there is the impression of an emotion, a state of mind, something internal which a person feels. Secondly, there are the external expressions or manifestations of the emotion in behaviour, including the person's statements, normally taken to be sincere, that he is feeling a particular emotion (or emotions). In relation to the example of Mary's sympathy for John, on the Humean analysis, we must distinguish between John's experience of sorrow (a particular impression, of a particular kind), his expression of sorrow through his behaviour, and Mary's awareness of John's sorrow. Since Mary has no direct access to John's felt experience of sorrow, her awareness of his sorrow is, on Hume's analysis, inferred from his behavioural expressions of sorrow. However, to enable us to say that Mary sympathises with John, her awareness of his sorrow must be converted or transformed from 'a lively idea' into an impression, that is, into Mary's felt experience of sorrow.

How, we may ask, is an idea 'presently converted into an impression, and acquires such a degree of force and vivacity, as to become the very passion itself and produce an equal emotion, as any original affection'?[17] However 'instantaneous this change of the idea into an impression may be, it proceeds from certain views and reflections, which will not escape the strict scrutiny of a philosopher, tho' they may the person himself, who makes them'.[18]

What are the 'certain views and reflections' which account, on Hume's view, for this instantaneous change? First, there is the fact that the impression of the self is 'always intimately present to us', giving rise to a lively conception of the self. This lively idea of the self in turn guarantees that we have a 'vivid conception' of every object related to us. The strength of the relation between an object and the self is a factor of two other types of relation, resemblance and contiguity. Of all the objects that can be so related by resemblance and contiguity to the self, none leads to a stronger relation than the passions or sentiments of others. The 'very remarkable resemblance' between the passions and sentiments of others and our own 'must very much contribute to make us enter into the sentiments of others, and embrace them with facility and pleasure'.[19] But resemblance is not the only relation which produces this effect for 'the sentiments of others have little influence when far removed from us, and require the relation of contiguity, to make them communicate themselves entirely'.[20] All these relations convey the impression of the self to the sentiments and passions of others and this 'makes us conceive them in the strongest and most lively manner'.

Secondly, whereas Hume thinks it is true, as set out in Book I of the *Treatise*, that 'all ideas are borrow'd from impressions, and that these two kinds of perceptions differ only in the degree of force or vivacity',[21] something almost amounting to the converse is expressed when Hume maintains that 'a lively idea of any object always approaches its impression'. In the case of sentiments and opinions, the lively idea 'approaches' so much to its impression that it can be converted to it. Since of all impressions the sentiments or passions depend more on the internal operations of the mind, they arise 'more naturally from the imagination and from every lively idea we form of them. This is the nature and cause of sympathy.'

Thirdly, the relation between cause and effect must be invoked in order to enable the observer to infer from the behaviour of the agent the kind of emotion he is experiencing, for this inference presupposes the validity of the claim that behavioural expressions of emotion are effects of which the cause is a felt, internal experience of the emotion. Here the inference is from cause to effect. It is possible also for the observer to infer from effect to cause in the sense that by observing a person in distressing circumstances, the observer infers that he is feeling sorrow.

The importance assigned by Hume to the causal relation in his account of sympathy is closely related to his basic epistemological presupposition that we can have only indirect and not direct knowledge of another's state of mind Thus the causal relation is a necessary condition of the notion of being able to have an idea (lively or otherwise) of another person's state of mind, and having a lively idea of another's state of mind is a necessary condition of sympathy. The relations of resemblance and contiguity function, it seems in Hume's account, as sufficient conditions of sympathy.

I wish now to comment on the inadequacies of Hume's analysis of sympathy. In doing so, I accept for the moment Hume's very questionable contention that 'sympathy' entails experiencing the same emotional experience as the person (or persons) sympathised with is experiencing.

1. It is possible to criticise Hume for assigning such an important role in his account of sympathy to the 'impression or consciousness of the self' on the grounds that in the first book of the *Treatise* he denies the existence of any such impression. To avoid a long digression into a discussion of Hume's views on self-identity, I propose to by-pass this problem, and assume that, for the purposes of his analysis of sympathy, his alleged inconsistency on the subject of the nature of the self can be satisfactorily resolved.

2. Hume's account of how sympathy is supposed to operate rests on one assertion which he is content to assert and does not discuss. If we grant Hume's epistemological claim that a 'lively idea of any object approaches its impression' ('approaches' here is a vague enough term, but that criticism can be discounted for the moment), what warrant is there for the claim that a lively idea of a passion approaches so much to its impression that it can be converted into it? This assumption is central to his account of the operation of sympathy, and yet it is based on a dubious assertion that emotions as objects of ideas enjoy a special status compared with the many other possible objects of ideas, e.g. tables, chairs and material objects in

general. Perhaps emotions do enjoy this special status, in that 'a lively idea' of an emotion is easily convertible into its impression, but Hume has not argued the point, he only states it. Moreover he has not supplied the criteria of what constitutes a 'lively idea', and yet it is crucially necessary for his account that he should do so, for it is precisely the lively idea of an emotion which is easily convertible into its impression. But when is an idea lively, thus satisfying the necessary condition which must be met before sympathy can occur?

3. From Hume's account it follows that for X to sympathise with Y it is necessary that X comes to feel the same emotion as Y, where Y feels his emotion temporally prior to X. Hume's reference to the sympathetic process being instantaneous seems to suggest he is thinking primarily of sympathy as a kind of immediate emotional reaction, as when we immediately begin to feel gay when we join what is already a gay party. It also allows for the case of someone coming to feel sorrow when he begins to realise another is sorrowful. Hume's account however does not seem to allow for the following two possible cases:

(i) X has lost his father whom he adores. Y despises X's father but, being X's friend, sympathises with him in his loss. Here 'sympathy' does not mean 'Y is feeling the same emotion as X', but is more like 'Y understands what it is for X to lose a father'.

(ii) The Principal in introducing the speaker, Sir John, to the audience, constantly refers to him as Mr John. The Principal is oblivious of his mistake. The audience increasingly feels embarrassed at the Principal's ineptitude.

Here sympathy entails feeling an emotion (granting for the moment that sympathy is an emotion) which the object of the sympathy does not feel: there is no emotion to be communicated on Hume's analysis. Hume seems to have realised that his account of sympathy in terms of the communication of emotion did not adequately deal with the phenomena covered by the word 'sympathy'. He was then forced to introduce a second principle or notion, that of contrast or comparison, which functions quite differently from the principle of communication. For instance one of Hume's examples is of the deep concern we feel for the infant prince of whom we know both that he is about to be murdered and that he is himself unaware of his impending fate. Such a person 'is more worthy of compassion the less sensible he is of his miserable condition'. We conceive of the misfortune of the young prince in the liveliest terms, and this contrasts most sharply with his feeling of security. Here there is no communication to us of what the prince feels, but by sympathy we imaginatively anticipate the fate of the prince, and feel pity for him. It hardly needs stressing that Hume's account of sympathy, based upon contrast or compassion, is hardly consistent with his earlier analysis in terms of communication.

On Hume's analysis of sympathy by communication, I sympathise with the man now suffering sorrow because of misfortune by sharing his feeling of sorrow. But in another of Hume's examples, if 'I saw a person perfectly unknown to me, who, while asleep in the fields, was in danger of being trod under foot by horses, I should immediately run to his assistance'.[22] In such a case I would be moved by sympathy based on the principle of comparison.

Thus sympathy can operate in relation to a present state of affairs or in relation to some anticipated, probable state of affairs. When I am sympathetically affected by another person's present or anticipated state of affairs, the influence on one need not be limited by consideration merely of his present state of affairs (e.g. misfortune) or by his future anticipated misfortune. When I consider his present (or future) misfortune, this 'diffuses its influence over all the related ideas, gives me a lively notion of all the circumstances of that person, whether past, present, or future; possible, probable, or certain. By means of this lively notion I am interested in them, take part with them; and feel a sympathetic motion in my breast, conformable to whatever I imagine in his.'[23] This 'lively notion of all the circumstances of another person' Hume calls 'extended sympathy', and it includes ideas of the person's good and bad, with the consequent experience of the passions appropriate to his good or evil. But this extended sympathy depends on the strength of the initial experience or impression (in Hume's terms) I get of the other person's misfortune. Granted that I experience a strong impression of another's uneasiness, this arouses feelings of pity in me, and of anger at those who did him wrong, and also of benevolence and love when I consider his good. 'Benevolence, therefore, arises from a great degree of misery, or any degree, strongly sympathised with.'[24] Thus 'the view of a city in ashes conveys benevolent sentiments; because we there enter so deep into the interests of the miserable inhabitants, as to wish for their prosperity, as well as feel their adversity'.[25] Finally Hume observes that this phenomenon of the double sympathy, and its tendency to cause love, may contribute 'to the production of the kindness, which we naturally bear our relations and acquaintance'.[26]

In the *Treatise* Hume distinguishes, as we have seen, between sympathy and benevolence. Sympathy is not a passion, although Hume does once refer to it as 'the communicated passion of sympathy',[27] which is presumably the only possible justification for MacNabb's classification of sympathy as 'another calm, regular and general passion'.[28] Benevolence on the other hand is one of the passions, not a 'pure emotion' like pride, but one, like love, which has associated with it a desire for the happiness of another.

The connection between sympathy and benevolence in Hume's account can be stated in relation to his two conceptions of sympathy. With regard to sympathy as communication, I can come to feel benevolent on observing another's benevolent feelings. In the case of sympathy as comparison, there is a much wider relation. By imaginative comparison of another's situation with my own, I consider all his circumstances, including what is for his good and what is not. In this comprehensive survey I am bound to feel benevolence since consideration of his good leads me to desire his happiness, as contemplation of what is harmful to him arouses my anger or even hatred. The double aspect of extended sympathy inevitably involves benevolence. Whereas Hume's notion of sympathy as communication of feeling is very limited and his account of its operation mechanical, his notion of extended sympathy brings in wider considerations, and not least the element of imaginative reconstruction of what is good or evil for another. "'Tis evident, that, in considering the future possible or probable condition of any person, we may enter into it with so vivid a conception as to make it our own concern; and by that means be sensible of pains and pleasures, which neither belong to ourselves, nor at the present instant have any real existence.'[29] But even in the notion of extended sympathy, Hume cannot release himself from the idea that to sympathise with someone or something (e.g. opinions) involves the sympathiser in experiencing 'impressions of pains and pleasures' which correspond with the impressions of pains and pleasures another is feeling, or would be feeling, if he knew all the sympathiser knows, as in Hume's example of our sympathy for the prince who is blissfully unaware of his impending execution. In analysing sympathy in a way that always and invariably involves sensible experiences of pleasures and pains, Hume is of course betraying once more the empiricist psychology to which he is committed.

4. *Benevolence and Justice*

In Book III of the *Treatise*, entitled 'Of Morals', Hume gives us his analysis of morality, which presupposes the validity of the psychological analysis of the passions in Book II.

At the beginning of Book III, under the title 'Of Virtue and Vice in General', Hume makes clear his empiricist presuppositions. Thus he writes:

> the chief spring or actuating principle of the human mind is pleasure or pain; and when these sensations are remov'd, both from our thought and feeling, we are, in a great measure, incapable of passion or action, of desire or volition.

And again:

> moral distinctions depend entirely on certain peculiar sentiments of pain and pleasure . . . whatever mental quality in ourselves or others gives us a satisfaction, by the survey or reflexion, is of course virtuous.[30]

Further assumptions made by Hume are implicit in the following quotations:

> the minds of all men are similar in their feelings and operations, nor can any one be actuated by any affection, of which all others are not, in some degree, susceptible. . . . No passion of another discovers itself immediately to the mind. We are only sensible of its causes or effects. From these we infer the passion. . . .[31]

Before proceeding to his analysis of morality, Hume touches briefly upon the similarity between the sentiments of beauty and those of morality. In one short paragraph,[32] he lays down several incompatible criteria of what gives rise to the sentiment of beauty. Amongst these are the following:

(*a*) any object which gives *pleasure to its possessor* is beautiful;

(*b*) any object which has a tendency to produce an effect, and that effect is (i) the *pleasure* or (ii) the *advantage* of *another person*, is beautiful;

(*c*) anything that is *useful* is beautiful;

(*d*) works of art, and 'productions of nature' are beautiful in proportion to '*their fitness for the use of man*';

(*e*) handsome and beautiful . . . is a quality . . . which has a tendency to produce an end that is *agreeable*.

In this section on Hume's discussion of benevolence and justice, we cannot pause to attempt to reconcile these apparently inconsistent criteria of the beautiful (italicised above). But since Hume holds that 'the same principle, in many instances, produces our sentiments of morals, as well as those of beauty',[33] we must be warned to expect a similar lack of precision in his analysis of morals.

Turning to Hume's analysis of virtue, we find that he divides virtue into the natural and the artificial. Since 'moral good and evil are certainly distinguished by our sentiments, and not by reason'[34] he argues that these sentiments of pleasure which are the basis of the virtues, and the sentiments of pain, the basis of the vices, arise either from (*a*) 'the mere species or appearance of characters or passions' or (*b*) 'reflexions on their tendency to the happiness of mankind, or of particular persons'.[35] Earlier, Hume states his criteria of what give rise to the moral sentiments in terms which differ slightly from (*b*) above, but which do not mention (*a*). Thus, 'moral distinctions arise, in a great measure, from the tendency of qualities or characters to the interests of society, our concern for that interest makes us approve or disapprove them'.[36] Here the point to notice is the slight difference between what tends to the *interests* of society, and the previous reference to what tends to the *happiness* of mankind. Hume's criteria are further complicated when he says that 'every quality of the mind is denominated virtuous, which gives pleasure by the mere survey', and this pleasure is said to have four sources, viz characters or qualities of character which are (i) 'naturally fitted to be useful to others, or to the person himself' or (ii) which are 'agreeable to others or to the person himself'.[37] Unfortunately Hume assumes that what is useful or agreeable to the self or to others is self-evident.

To account for the existence of many of the natural virtues, Hume appeals to the existence of qualities 'which acquire approbation because of their tendency to the good of mankind';[38] such virtues are 'meekness, beneficence, charity, generosity, clemency, moderation, equity'. The artificial virtues are so because their advantage to society is established by connection, and then upheld, or supported, through sympathy, by a natural sentiment.[39] Apart from being established by convention, another difference between a natural and an artificial virtue is said to arise from the fact that good ensues from each instance of the natural virtue, but this is not necessarily so of the artificial virtue. Hume illustrates this by reference to justice, for a single act of justice may not be advantageous to society, whereas the whole system of justice is advantageous. Each virtue – even benevolence, justice, gratitude, integrity – 'excites a different sentiment or feeling in the spectator'.[40]

When we turn back to Part II of Book III for Hume's discussion of justice and injustice, which follows his chapter 'Of Virtue and Vice in General', he begins the discussion by laying down as axiomatic that

1. Actions are virtuous in so far as they spring from motives that are virtuous.

Here Hume adopts the view that the externally observable behavioural part of an action is not the object of moral assessment. 'The external performance has no merit.'[41] What is judged to be morally good or bad is the motive from which the action springs, and by virtue of which the action is made good or bad. Hume does not therefore draw the modern distinction between the rightness or wrongness of the act, the observable behaviour and the goodness or badness of the motive to which we turn for an assessment of the moral worth of the agent.

2. That regard to the virtue of an action cannot be 'the first motive for its performance'. As Hume puts it: 'that no action can be virtuous, or morally good, unless there be in human nature some motive to produce it distinct from the sense of its morality.'[42] If actions are regarded as signs indicating the nature of the agent's character, then an awareness of the morality of an action cannot be the first motive of an action,

since, according to Hume, actions can only be motivated by sentiments or passions, that is, by a natural motive.

If actions can only be motivated by natural motives how can we account for just actions, since clearly justice is not one of the natural motives? Hume considers possible natural motives, for instance self-interest, only to reject them. Thus self-interest cannot be the motive for justice because a particular just action, abstracted from the system of justice, may be contrary to one's private interest, and indeed self-love is the source of all manner of injustices and violence. Another possible candidate is 'regard to the publick interest'. Hume rejects it for three reasons. First, public interest is not 'naturally attached' to the observation of the rules of justice but is only connected to it by a 'convention'. Since Hume wishes to demonstrate that justice is in fact based on convention, he asserts, somewhat vaguely, that the observation of the rules of justice and the public interest are not 'naturally attached'. Secondly, if we suppose a secret transaction, e.g. borrowing money, where the effects of the action concern only the persons concerned, then the public has no interest in the matter, and the obligation to fulfil the transaction (that is, repay the loan) could be regarded as removed if the motive to justice was in fact regard for the public interest. But since we do not believe that the obligation to fulfil the transaction is removed, even in the case of a secret transaction, then the motive for fulfilling the obligation cannot be regard to the public interest. Thirdly, people do not have regard to the public interest when they do what is just, e.g. repay loans or keep promises. As Árdal points out, this last point does not show that 'the public interest may not ultimately be the source of the obligation to be just'.[43] Hume believes that regard for the public interest, or 'extensive benevolence', is 'too remote and too sublime to affect the generality of mankind', and cannot thus be strong enough to counteract selfishness, as must be the case with just actions, since injustice would so often be to our selfish gain. 'There is no such passion in human minds, as the love of mankind, merely as such, independent of personal qualities, of services, or of relation to ourself.'[44] Hume cannot therefore appeal to extensive benevolence as the motive of justice, for he simply denies its existence. On the whole, men's passions motivate them to actions which are in their selfish interest. In the case of the other-regarding passions – 'love, compassion, gratitude, friendship, liberality, zeal, fidelity' – the very close relations established between the self and the other person (or persons) who are the objects of these passions militate obviously against the strict claims of justice. We are likely to be biased against the requirements of justice in favour of those whom we love. By means of the principle of sympathy men do however, according to Hume, act benevolently towards strangers, 'those who are not our friends or relations'. Here the strength of the benevolence rests on the degree of closeness of the relation (not in itself very close) to the stranger. It varies in strength from the moderately strong to the very weak. It cannot therefore be a universal motive for justice. In any case, limited benevolence, operating through sympathy, influences our behaviour both to men and to animals, whereas justice, according to Hume, only concerns our relations with men, and not with the brutes. We may be unkind to animals, implies Hume, but we cannot be unjust. The reason for this seems to be that we cannot establish with animals the kind of convention required to bring the system of justice as a whole into existence.[45]

'Private benevolence' or 'regard to the interests' of the parties concerned would frequently lead to unjust acts.

> For what if he be my enemy, and has given me just cause to hate him? What if he be a vicious man, and deserves the hatred of all mankind? What if he be a miser, and can make no use of what I would deprive him of? What if he be a profligate debauchee, and would rather receive harm than benefit from large possessions? What if I be in necessity, and have urgent motives to acquire something to my family? In all these cases, the original motive to justice would fail; and consequently the justice itself, and along with it all property, right and obligation.[46]

Hume concludes that private benevolence is not the original motive of justice.

From his review of the possible natural motives for justice, Hume concludes that 'the sense of justice and injustice is not deriv'd from nature, but arises artificially, tho' necessarily from education, and human conventions'.[47] He then sets out to answer two questions, firstly, how the convention on which justice is based arose from motives that are natural, and secondly, how justice came to be regarded as a virtue. Of these two questions, the first is more directly relevant to this section on Hume's views concerning the relation between justice and benevolence.

In answering the first question, it must be noted that Hume sets out to give what he considers to be an intelligible account of the origin of justice. He does not pretend to give an account which is factual and historical. Indeed the necessary evidence for such an historical account did not exist in Hume's day, when the study of history as a systematic reconstruction of the past was in its infancy. That evidence may still not be available today.

In his attempt to produce an intelligible account of the origin of justice, Hume considers several relevant factors. Man possesses many wants and needs, but is ill-equipped by nature to satisfy them. He soon realises that by co-operation with others he can better provide for his needs and wants. Thus by mutual co-operation with others, man's power over nature is increased: division of labour in society leads to the acquisition of specialised skills and co-operation better enables men to counter natural hazards and accidents. Man thus becomes aware that society is to his advantage, and to this extent, the impulse to form society is based firmly on self-interest, which is natural. It is also based on another 'original motive', namely 'the natural appetite between the sexes', which is the basis for the family. The institution of the family teaches men and women to co-operate with each other in the nurture of offspring. Here, within the family, there is scope for generosity, especially between parents and their children, so that Hume must deny that men are solely and irredeemably selfish.

> I am sensible, that, generally speaking, the representations of this quality [selfishness] have been carried much too far; and that the descriptions, which certain philosophers delight so much to form of mankind in this particular, are as wide of nature as any accounts of monsters, which we meet with in fables and romances. So far from thinking, that men have no affection for any thing beyond themselves, I am of opinion, that tho' it be rare to meet with one, who loves any single person better than himself; yet 'tis as rare to meet with one, in whom all the kind affections, taken together, do not over-balance all the selfish.[48]

This generosity does not normally extend beyond one's family, and the very zeal with which a man wants to do the best he can for members of his family leads inevitably to conflict with others who share the same aim for their families. This conflict is intensified because of 'a peculiarity in our outward circumstances', that is our enjoyment of such possessions as we 'have acquired by our industry and good fortune'. The need to protect our possessions which are most vulnerable to attack because of the envy of those who lack possessions, is one of the preconditions for establishing the conventions on which the system of justice is based. Another is the relative scarcity of the goods available for distribution between individuals. One of the conventions on which justice is founded is the individual's recognition that it is in his interest to leave another safely in the possession of his goods provided the other person will act in a like manner towards his own goods. The acquisitive desire is so powerful in each individual that if it were not restrained by the rules of justice, it would certainly destroy society. 'This avidity alone, of acquiring goods and possessions for ourselves and our nearest friends is insatiable, perpetual, universal and directly destructive of society.'[49] There is no affection in the human breast which can quell this love of gain. Certainly the benevolence we feel towards strangers is too weak. The only thing that can restrain the acquisitive impulse is the system of the rules of justice. Justice is thus based on human conventions designed to remedy the selfishness of human nature with its great generosity to members of one's own immediate family, and its limited generosity to strangers on the one hand, and the scarcity of goods with which to satisfy the individual's wants and needs on the other. From Hume's analysis it follows that if extensive benevolence prevailed, or if there were a superabundance of goods to satisfy the wants and needs of each individual, there would be no need for the system of justice.

As for Hume's second question, how does justice come to be regarded as a virtue, Hume implies that since justice ultimately owes its origin to self-interest, so sympathy with the public interest is the source of that 'moral approbation which attends that virtue'.

It is reasonably clear from Hume's account of the origin of justice that the root of the conventions necessary for the system of justice to be established is the recognition that co-operation between individuals in society is to each other's interest. In short the ultimate ground of justice is self-interest, and in maintaining this view, Hume is in effect reducing justice to prudence. Closely connected with this is his assumption that men are by nature capable only of limited benevolence. They are naturally generous to their relatives and friends but to others benevolence is weak. The other main condition which gives rise to justice on Hume's view is the scarcity of goods and possessions. Hume states categorically that if goods were superabundant, there would be no need for the rules of justice. But scarcity of goods for distribution is only a necessary condition of the need for the conventions leading to justice. A sufficient condition is that men are selfishly acquisitive by nature. In a world where men are not acquisitive by nature, the system of justice might not be necessary, even granted a relative scarcity of goods for distribution. That men are selfishly acquisitive by nature, so much so that their acquisitive impulses can destroy society unless kept in check by the system of justice, is an assumption which Hume states and does not argue for. It is the corner stone of his analysis of justice. A disagreement between Hume and a non-Humean who holds that men are not selfish by nature, but are made so by the rules and conventions of society, is not a conceptual disagreement concerning the analysis of justice. It is a disagreement in ethical attitudes. To say that men are selfishly acquisitive by nature is not to state a fact, as Hume would have us believe, but is an expression of a moral attitude.

In his discussion of the origins of the system of justice, Hume rejects as fanciful the view that there ever existed a state of nature preceding society in which the rules of justice were unknown. He seems to reject such a view on the grounds that we lack any historical evidence of its existence. Hume does not seem to have realised that the very conception of a state of nature (that is, of individuals living independently and in complete isolation from each other, thus constituting a historical phase prior to the existence of society) raises acute conceptual difficulties. The crucial objection to any such notion is not so much that we do not possess reliable historical evidence of the existence of the state of nature as that the notion is itself incoherent.

If the question is asked whether there existed a state of nature in which men were universally benevolent, and in which the rules of justice were not required, Hume in effect replies by maintaining that we have no evidence to support the contention that there ever existed such a state of nature. Now if the notion of a state of nature preceding society is incoherent, so similarly the notion of a universal benevolence in such a state of nature is incoherent. However, it is still possible to ask the question which Hume's assumptions do not allow him to ask, namely, is it possible to conceive of a society in which men are universally benevolent? It is surely possible to answer this question affirmatively. One could then ask whether the rules of justice would be necessary in a society of universally benevolent individuals. Hume of course has not raised, let alone discussed, such a question.

Hume's analysis of justice in terms of self-interest and limited benevolence makes justice, as we have already observed, a form of prudence. His estimate of man's capacity for only limited benevolence makes it impossible that the motive of justice is benevolence. In any case justice is a distinct and separate virtue from either prudence or benevolence. The truly just man is the person who acts justly out of regard for justice itself and not from motives of benevolence or providence. In attempting to interpret justice in terms ultimately of prudence, combined with limited benevolence, Hume's analysis suffers from several weaknesses, not least his artificial distinction between natural and artificial virtues. Far from being removed, these weaknesses are underlined when we recognise that Hume argues from a moral standpoint centred on what his opponents would claim is a biased view of human nature, of man as capable only of limited benevolence. Hume is entitled to hold this view of human nature, reflecting as it seems to do the values of the property-owning bourgeois of eighteenth-century Britain, but in conceding this right we should not be misled into thinking that Hume's view of human nature is the necessary starting point for a conceptual analysis of justice.

Conclusion

The foregoing survey of the views of Hutcheson, Butler and Hume on the subject of benevolence highlights the fact that these three philosophers, not unnaturally, share certain epistemological, psychological and metaphysical standpoints. By way of a concluding comment on this survey I propose very briefly to consider each of these standpoints.

1. All three refer to benevolence as an affection or passion. In general, 'affection' and 'passion' are their eighteenth-century terms for what we call emotions or feelings. They tend to use these terms in a very wide sense to cover such diverse states of minds as wishes, desires, emotions and passions – that is, 'passion' in the narrow sense of a highly charged emotion, e.g. rage. Their account of how these states of mind of affections or passions come to exist, or can exist, in the human mind presupposes, in general, a Lockean empiricist epistemology, even though this epistemology owes in turn a great deal to Cartesian presuppositions. To the extent that the Cartesian dualism of mind and matter can no longer be accepted, at least in its Cartesian form, to that extent the Lockean epistemology developed upon Cartesian premises must be rejected. This undermines the basic epistemological standpoints of Hutcheson, Butler and Hume. So far as the analysis of the emotions or feelings is concerned, the main weakness of a Lockean standpoint derives from regarding an emotion as an item in consciousness the description of which is externally, and therefore contingently, related to its object. This leads Hume to assert, as we have seen, that the effects of love might, contingently, have been those of hatred. Such a phenomenon is logically, and not contingently, impossible, for if there existed an emotion with the effects of hatred, either this emotion is hatred or else we could not understand or make sense of any other description of it.

2. Moving from epistemology to psychology, eighteenth-

century philosophy in general adopted a view concerning the motivation of human actions, and in particular of moral actions, which is very evident in the moral philosophy of Hutcheson and Hume and, to a lesser degree, in that of Butler. This was the view that human actions, in the sense of deliberate, intentional actions, are always motivated by some desire or inclination, and that in the absence of any such desire or inclination, any rational recognition or awareness of what is to be done is impotent to motivate action. There are several affections or feelings which can motivate action, but self-love and benevolence are the most important. Hutcheson argues for the pre-eminence of benevolence, and in particular maintains that virtue is based upon the motive or affection of benevolence. On Hume's psychological analysis, actions are motivated by a number of emotions and passions, and so far as moral actions are concerned, benevolence is not the only motive for virtue. Butler's position is not so clear cut. In the main he adopts a psychological position akin to that of Hutcheson and Hume, that is, actions are motivated by the 'appetites, passions, and affections', and benevolence is clearly included in this class of feelings or emotions. However, if one asks what is the motive of virtuous actions, in some contexts Butler gives an answer which agrees with Hutcheson's, namely, the supreme moral motive is benevolence. In other contexts, where he brings in his doctrine of conscience, Butler seems to imply that our awareness or recognition of what is our duty is itself sufficient to motivate our action, though failure to do our duty is attributable to the superior pressure or strength of powerful desires or feelings which succeed in motivating actions which are contrary to what conscience commands.

This eighteenth-century analysis of moral actions in terms of their motivation by certain feelings or emotions finds an echo in the preoccupation of contemporary moral philosophy with attempts to produce an emotivist analysis of morality, although modern emotivism differs in many respects from eighteenth-century moral philosophy, not least in its concern to analyse moral statements as expressions of emotion, and its lack of interest in the question of the psychological role of the emotions as springs of action. Many philosophers who are otherwise sympathetic to some kind of emotivist analysis of ethics are unable to accept the particular emotivist theories of Ayer and

Stevenson, largely because these theories seem to ground morality on feelings or emotions which cannot be influenced by reason or understanding, thus making morality subjective and non-rational. It is therefore suggested that it is more fruitful to concentrate on the attempt to analyse moral concepts and moral statements in terms of attitudes, for thereby the rationality and objectivity of ethics can be re-instated. Its rationality can be re-instated because it is possible to develop the notion of appealing to reasons that justify this or that attitude, and objectivity can be restored by insisting that morality is based on emotional attitudes shared in common by individuals by virtue of their membership of a particular society.

Both of these notions of the rationality and objectivity of ethics appear in the eighteenth century, and so its philosophical discussions of them may be of particular relevance for some trends in contemporary moral philosophy. For although the eighteenth-century philosophers we have examined insist that actions can only be motivated by passions and affections, they do not always and unambiguously insist that there are pure feelings which cannot be influenced by rational reflection. For example in Butler's argument rational reflection, it seems, can reinforce the affection of benevolence so that what may occur as an impulse can develop into a settled disposition of character. Even though Hume did write that 'reason is, and ought only to be, the slave of the passions', he nevertheless, and perhaps not altogether consistently, assigns a place to rational reflection in the role that the imagination plays in the operations of sympathy; in considering how we should act for the good of another, we must not only consider the other person's circumstances but must reflect upon such other factors as his circumstances in the past, his qualities of character, and the probable effect of his present circumstances on his future state.

Objectivity, more so than rationality, figures prominently in eighteenth-century discussions. Whatever the philosophical weakness of their analysis of moral concepts and of moral statements, Hutcheson, Butler and Hume were in no doubt that morality was concerned with certain 'objective' features of experience, and not with the purely subjective expression of the attitudes and feelings of individuals.

Although eighteenth-century philosophical discussions on

moral topics are of unquestionable value and interest, recent discussions in the field of modern philosophical psychology have made evident the weaknesses and inadequacies of its eighteenth-century counterpart. Some of these weaknesses can be briefly mentioned.

As we have already seen, in analysing the motives of moral action, eighteenth-century philosophers are, in general, content to operate with a conceptual framework in which the appetites, passions and affections occupy a central position. However, as a description of a general class of feelings or emotions which operate as motives of actions, the terms 'appetite', 'passion' and 'affection' are far too imprecise and vague to do the job for which they are required. We need to distinguish as carefully and as precisely as possible between such different mental states as desires, wants, wishes, attitudes and passions, all of which can be included in the class of feelings or emotions that motivate action. Moreover the important element of belief involved in these mental states, and their possible ordering in a hierarchy[1] (ranging from, for instance, on the one hand attitudes, which involve relations to several beliefs, to passion, which may include no belief at all) are completely overlooked by eighteenth-century moral philosophy.

The important topic of the relation between an emotion and its object is also inadequately discussed. Hutcheson, Butler and Hume distinguish, though not explicitly, between the formal and the material objects of an emotion, but they do not seem to make further distinctions between notional and intentional objects. The real object is the object towards which a man's emotion is directed. Thus if Jones feels compassion for Smith, then there must be something to which his compassion is directed, and that is something about Smith's circumstances, which are in some way distressing. The formal object of the emotion is the description of the kind of thing under which the description of the object of the emotion must fall if it is to count as an object of that emotion. Thus the formal object of compassion is what is distressing. The notional object is given by the description under which the subject sees the object of his emotion as he believes it to be. Thus an emotion may be based on error. Jones may wrongly believe that Smith's circumstances are distressing, but Jones's belief that Smith's circumstances are distressing is the notional object of Jones's compassion. Intentional objects are propositions which enter into mental states in so far as these include beliefs.

A fuller analysis of benevolence than is to be found in eighteenth-century philosophy might profitably apply this four-fold distinction to a discussion of the object of benevolence.[2]

As for the actual analysis of benevolence advanced by Hutcheson, Butler and Hume, all three agree that the formal object of benevolence lies in seeking the good of another, and by this good is understood his happiness. Furthermore they seem agreed that the advancement of the happiness of another is brought about either by an action whose aim is positively to increase the happiness of another or by an action whose aim is positively to reduce the misery or unhappiness of another. With regard to the former, Hume explores the part played by sympathy in the notion of positively seeking to achieve the happiness of another, while Butler examines compassion: together they serve to uncover some of the complex character of benevolence. But there are elements in its complexity which have been overlooked. For example, can a man best promote the happiness of his fellows by working silently for ends he can never hope to see realised, or by working for and amongst persons for whom he does not feel, and cannot feel, affection, or by doing what must alienate or grieve those whom he loves best, or in ways which make it necessary for him to dispense with the most intimate of human ties.[3] In other words, benevolence can find expression in a variety of ways, and not all of these have been explored by Hutcheson, Butler and Hume.

The question whether it is possible to act benevolently towards persons for whom we can feel no affection leads one to challenge the central assumption of eighteenth-century moral philosophy, namely that benevolence is an emotion. If benevolence is an emotion, then it follows that we cannot feel or summon up this emotion at will, and the presence in us of this motivating principle of actions which do good to others is a contingent matter, on which we can hardly base morality, as Balguy points out in his criticism of Hutcheson.[4] And if benevolence is not an emotion, then it may be the case that benevolent actions of doing good to others can be motivated by a recognition or realisation that so acting for the good of others is our duty. But to argue this is to challenge Hume's claim that action can only be motivated by passion, as it is also to move in the direction of Kant's claim that doing good to others from benevolent feelings or inclinations merits our approval but not our *moral* approval.

3. In addition to their epistemological and psychological assumptions, eighteenth-century discussions of benevolence possess also metaphysical implications, a point perhaps worth noting in an age which seeks to discuss ethics divorced from metaphysics. Both Hutcheson and Butler – the latter much more evidently so than the former – discuss benevolence in the context of an analysis of human nature, and both assert that the human nature in which benevolence exists has been created by God. Analysing a particular moral concept in relation to a whole scheme of moral concepts, which in turn are linked to certain theological assertions, is the kind of thing meant by saying that ethics is discussed in a metaphysical context. In contrast Hume notoriously leaves God out of the picture, and is content to analyse benevolence as one of the natural virtues which belong to the essential nature of man. It might seem then that Hume has no metaphysical axe to grind, and that he is not vulnerable to the charge that can be levelled against Hutcheson and Butler, namely that their analysis of benevolence as a God-given virtue, necessary to the nature of man in order to fulfil God's overall design, rests ultimately on an unproven theological assertion. But is Hume's analysis so free of metaphysical overtones? Hume's moral standpoint centres on the belief that man is capable only of limited benevolence. What is the status of this assertion? If it is based on observation, it is, if true, contingently true, and the future may falsify it; in that case, Hume's analysis of morality is rendered valueless. Hume could hardly have meant his assertion to be taken as true by definition, as part of what we mean by the term 'man'. If it is neither contingently true, nor true by definition, the claim that man is capable of only limited benevolence seems to be a metaphysical claim, no less so, and no more so than Butler's claim that God created man with the capacity to act benevolently in order thereby to fulfil his purpose for the creation. How one can resolve conflicting metaphysical claims such as those of Butler and Hume is a question which certainly warrants careful discussion, but is one that falls outside the scope of this essay.

Notes

Chapter 1

1. The view that simple ideas derive *indirectly* from sense impressions leads to the 'moral sentiment' view. See Raphael, *The Moral Sense*, chapter 1.

2. See Norman Kemp Smith, *The Philosophy of David Hume* (London. Macmillan 1941), chapter 2.

3. See Raphael, *Moral Sense*, chapter 1.

4. 'That as the Author of Nature has determin'd us to receive, by our external senses, pleasant or disagreeable ideas of objects, according as they are useful or hurtful to our bodies. . . .' *Inquiry*, 4th ed., I viii, p. 128.

5. *Inquiry*, I viii, p. 129.

6. *Inquiry*, II i, p. 132.

7. *Inquiry*, II ii, p. 134.

8. *Inquiry*, II ii, p. 135.

9. *Inquiry*, II ii, p. 135.

10. *Inquiry*, III viii, p. 181.

11. *Inquiry*, I, p. 115.

12. *Inquiry*, II ix, p. 183.

13. *Inquiry*, III x, p. 184.

14. *Inquiry*, II iv, p. 139.

15. *Inquiry*, II iv, p. 142.

16. *Inquiry*, II vii, pp. 152–3.

17. *Inquiry*, III xi, p. 187.

18. *Inquiry*, II iii, p. 137.

19. *Inquiry*, II iv, p. 138.

20. *Inquiry*, II iv, p. 140.

21. *Inquiry*, II iv, p. 141.

22. *Inquiry*, II iv, p. 142.

23. *Inquiry*, II iv, pp. 143–4.

24. *Inquiry*, II iv, p. 139.

25. *Inquiry*, II v, p. 146.

26. 'Reflecting on our own minds again will best discover the truth.' *Inquiry*, II v, p. 146.

27. *Inquiry*, III xi, p. 188.

28. *Inquiry*, III iv, p. 175.

29. *Inquiry*, III v, pp. 175–6.

30. *Inquiry*, I i, p. 113.

31. *Inquiry*, I iv, p. 118.

32. *Inquiry*, I iii, p. 116.

33. *Inquiry*, I iii, p. 117.

34. *Inquiry*, I v, p. 120.
35. *Inquiry*, I v, p. 122.
36. *Inquiry*, I vi, p. 124.
37. *Inquiry*, I vi, p. 126.
38. *Inquiry*, I viii, pp. 128–9.

Chapter 2

1. A. Duncan-Jones, *Butler's Moral Philosophy* (London 1952), p. 35.
2. *Fifteen Sermons*, Preface, § xii, p. 4. (All references are to the author's edition of Butler's *Fifteen Sermons* (London: S.P.C.K. 1970). The number of the sermon is given in arabic numerals and the paragraphs in roman numbering.)
3. *Sermons*, 3 ix, p. 39.
4. *Sermons*, 2 x, p. 31.
5. *Sermons*, 2 i, p. 27.
6. *Sermons*, 4 vii, p. 43.
7. *Sermons*, 2 x, p. 31.
8. *Sermons*, 2 xv, p. 33.
9. C. D. Broad, *Five Types of Ethical Theory* (London 1930), p. 57.
10. A. Duncan-Jones, *Butler's Moral Philosophy*, p. 45, and T. H. McPherson, 'The Development of Bishop Butler's Ethics', part 1, *Philosophy*, XXIII (1948), p. 321.
11. *Sermons*, 5 iii, p. 52.
12. *Sermons*, 6 ix, p. 61.
13. Duncan-Jones *Butler's Moral Philosophy*, pp. 48–9.
14. *Sermons*, 6 i, p. 57.
15. *Sermons*, 9 ix, p. 83.
16. *Sermons*, 6 ix, p. 61.
17. Duncan-Jones, *Butler's Moral Philosophy*, p. 45.
18. F. Hutcheson, *An Essay on the Nature and Conduct of the Passions and Affections, with Illustrations on the Moral Sense*, 3rd ed. (1730), p. 29.
19. Hutcheson, *Essay*, p. 64.
20. *Sermons*, 13 iii, p. 123.
21. *Sermons*, 5 i, p. 50 note.
22. *Sermons*, 5 iii, p. 51.
23. *Sermons*, 5 iii, p. 51.
24. *Sermons*, 1 viii, p. 21.
25. *Sermons*, 1 viii, p. 22.
26. *Sermons*, 13 vii, p. 125.
27. *Sermons*, 12 xi, p. 115.
28. *Butler's Moral Philosophy*, p. 45.
29. *Sermons*, 1 xiv, p. 25.
30. *Sermons*, Preface xxxxi, p. 15.
31. *Sermons*, 11 v, p. 100.
32. *Sermons*, 1 vi, p. 20.
33. *Sermons*, 11 xi, p. 103.
34. *Sermons*, 12 xi, p. 115.
35. *Sermons*, 12 iii, p. 111.

36. *Sermons*, 12 iii, p. 112.
37. See above, p. 49.
38. *Sermons*, 5 x, p. 54.
39. *Sermons*, 12 xxvii, p. 119.
40. These are in Sermon 11, paras xi, xii, xiii, xvii and xix.
41. *Sermons*, Preface xiv, p. 6.
42. *Sermons*, 3 ii, p. 35.
43. *Sermons*, 3 ii, p. 35.
44. *Sermons*, 2 viii, p. 31.
45. *Sermons*, 2 iii, p. 28.
46. *Sermons*, 2 ix, p. 31.
47. *Sermons*, 3 ix, p. 39.
48. See above, p. 15.
49. *Sermons*, 12 xxxii, p. 121.
50. One of the most important references to this point is to be found in Sermon 11, devoted largely to discussing self-love. Butler writes, 'Every particular affection, benevolence among the rest, is subservient to self-love by being the instrument of private enjoyment.' *Sermons*, 11 xix, p. 109.
51. *Sermons*, 12 iii, p. 112.
52. *Sermons*, 12 iii, p. 112.
53. *Sermons*, 12 vii, p. 113.
54. *Sermons*, 12 vii, p. 113.
55. *Sermons*, 11 xv, p. 106.
56. *Sermons*, 11 xv, p. 106.
57. *Sermons*, 11 xvi, p. 107.
58. *Sermons*, 1 vi, p. 20.
59. *Sermons*, Preface xxxviii, p. 14.
60. *Sermons*, 12 xxi, p. 117.
61. *Sermons*, 12 xxv, f.
62. *Sermons*, 12 xxvii, p. 119.
63. *Sermons*, 12 xii, p. 115.
64. *Sermons*, 12 xiv, p. 115.
65. *Sermons*, 5 i, p. 50 note.
66. *Sermons*, 5 i, p. 50 note.
67. *Sermons*, 5 viii, p. 54.
68. *Sermons*, 5 xii, p. 55.
69. *Sermons*, 6 ix, p. 61.
70. *Sermons*, 1 vi, p. 19.
71. *Sermons*, 1 vi, p. 19 note.
72. *Dissertation*, § 8, p. 152.
73. *Dissertation*, § 8, p. 152.
74. *Dissertation*, § 8, p. 152.
75. *Dissertation*, § 8, p. 152.
76. T. H. McPherson, in *Philosophy* (1948).
77. Broad, *Five Types of Ethical Theory*, chapter 3.
78. A. E. Taylor, 'Some Features of Butler's Ethics' in *Philosophical Studies* (London, 1934).
79. *Sermons*, 2 viii, p. 31.

80. My italics.
81. *Sermons*, 11 ix, pp. 101–2.

Chapter 3

1. But see Anthony Flew, *Hume's Philosophy of Belief* (London 1961).
2. Book II, Part 3 Section iii.
3. p. 417. (All page-references are to L. A. Selby-Bigge's edition of the *Treatise* (Oxford 1902).)
4. *Treatise*, II 3 iii, 'On the Influencing Motives of the Will', the section which includes the celebrated sentence, 'Reason is, and ought only to be, the slave of the passions, and can never pretend to any other office than to serve and obey them.' (p. 415).
5. Compare Pall S. Árdal, *Passion and Value in Hume's Treatise* (Edinburgh 1966), pp. 18–19.
6. J. A. Passmore, *Hume's Intention* (London 1968), p. 109.
7. *Treatise*, II 2 i, p. 329.
8. *Treatise*, II 2 i, p. 329.
9. *Treatise*, II 2 i, p. 331.
10. *Treatise*, II 2 iv, p. 352.
11. *Treatise*, II 2 iv, p. 352.
12. Book II Part 2 of the *Treatise*.
13. *Treatise*, II 2 vi, p. 367.
14. *Treatise*, II 2 vi, p. 366.
15. *Treatise*, II 2 vi, p. 368.
16. *Treatise*, II 2 ix, pp. 385–6.
17. *Treatise*, II 1 xi, p. 317.
18. *Treatise*, II 1 xi, p. 317.
19. *Treatise*, II 1 xi, p. 318.
20. *Treatise*, II 1 xi, p. 318.
21. *Treatise*, II 1 xi, p. 319.
22. *Treatise*, II 2 ix, p. 385.
23. *Treatise*, II 2 ix, p. 386.
24. *Treatise*, II 2 ix, p. 387.
25. *Treatise*, II 2 ix, p. 388.
26. *Treatise*, II 2 ix, p. 389.
27. *Treatise*, II 2 vii, p. 370.
28. *David Hume's Theory of Knowledge and Morality*, p. 166.
29. *Treatise*, II 2 ix, p. 386.
30. *Treatise*, III 3 i, p. 574.
31. *Treatise*, III 3 i, pp. 575–6.
32. *Treatise*, III 3 i, p. 576.
33. *Treatise*, III 3 i, p. 577.
34. *Treatise*, III 3 i, p. 589.
35. *Treatise*, III 3 i, p. 589.
36. *Treatise*, III 3 i, p. 579.
37. *Treatise*, III 3 i, p. 591.
38. *Treatise*, III 3 i, p. 578.
39. *Treatise*, III 3 i, p. 578.

40. *Treatise*, III 3 iv, p. 607.
41. *Treatise*, III 2 i, p. 477.
42. *Treatise*, III 2 i, p. 479.
43. Árdal, *Passion and Value*, p. 172.
44. *Treatise*, III 2 i, p. 481.
45. See further Árdal, *Passion and Value*, p. 174.
46. *Treatise*, III 2 i, p. 482.
47. *Treatise*, III 2 i, p. 483.
48. *Treatise*, III 2 ii, pp. 486–7.
49. *Treatise*, III 2 ii, pp. 491–2.

Chapter 4

1. This suggestion is made by Roger Scruton in his article 'Attitudes, Beliefs and Reasons' in *Morality and Moral Reasoning*, ed. Casey (London 1971), p. 38.

2. I am indebted to Scruton for this distinction (in *Morality and Moral Reasoning*).

3. These examples are taken from Sidgwick, *The Methods of Ethics* (London: Macmillan 1907), Book I.

4. John Balguy, 'The Foundation of Moral Goodness', in *British Moralists, 1650–1800*, ed. D. D. Raphael (Oxford 1969), I 289–403.

Bibliography

I – Texts

Butler, J., *Fifteen Sermons* and *Dissertation upon the Nature of Virtue*, ed. T. A. Roberts, London 1970.

Clarke, S., *A Discourse Concerning the Being and Attributes of God, and Obligations of Natural Religion*, 1706.

Hume, David, *A Treatise of Human Nature*, ed. L. A. Selby-Bigge, Oxford 1888 repr. 1967.

Enquiries Concerning the Human Understanding and Concerning the Principles of Morals, ed. L. A. Selby-Bigge, Oxford 1902.

Hutcheson, F., *An Inquiry Concerning Moral Good and Evil*, London 1725.

An Essay on the Nature and Conduct of the Passions and Affections, 1728.

Illustrations Upon the Moral Sense, 1728.

Shaftesbury, Earl of, *Enquiry Concerning Virtue or Merit*, 1699.

II – Books on Hutcheson, Butler and Hume

Árdal, P. S., *Passion and Value in Hume's Treatise*, Edinburgh 1966.

Basson, A. H., *David Hume*, London 1958.

Broad, C. D., *Five Types of Ethical Theory*, London 1930.

Broiles, R. D., *The Moral Philosophy of David Hume*, The Hague 1964.

Chappell, V. C. (ed.), *Hume*, London 1958.

Duncan-Jones, A., *Butler's Moral Philosophy*, Pelican 1952.

Flew, Antony, *Hume's Philosophy of Belief*, London 1961.

Hendel, Charles W., *Studies in the Philosophy of David Hume*, Indianapolis 1963.

Kemp, J., *Reason, Action and Morality*, London 1964.

Kydd, Rachel M., *Reason and Conduct in Hume's Treatise*, London 1946.

Mackinnon, D. M., *A Study in Ethical Theory*, London 1957.

MacNabb, D. G. C., *David Hume: His Theory of Knowledge and Morality*, London 1951.

Martineau, J., *Types of Ethical Theory*, Oxford 1901.

Mercer, Philip, *Sympathy and Ethics*, Oxford 1972.

Passmore, J. E., *Hume's Intentions*, Cambridge 1952.

Ralph Cudworth, Cambridge 1951.

Pears, D. F. (ed.), *David Hume: a Symposium*, London 1963.

Prior, A. N., *Logic and the Basis of Ethics*, Oxford 1949.

Raphael, D. D., *The Moral Sense*, London 1947.

RASHDALL, H., *The Theory of Good and Evil*, Oxford 1907.

SCOTT, W. R., *Francis Hutcheson*, Cambridge 1900.

SESONSKE, A. and FLEMING, N. (ed.), *Human Understanding: Studies in the Philosophy of David Hume*, Belmont 1965.

SMITH, Norman Kemp, *The Philosophy of David Hume*, London 1941.

STEWART, J. B., *The Moral and Political Philosophy of David Hume*, New York 1963.